Paul.

Every best wish

Reading this might
build some bridges.!!

David.

G000096200

Gordon Hannon

Some Parson! Some Man.

A Biography

By

David Hannon

Published by Drumilly Books

© DAVID HANNON   2004

The right of David Hannon to be identified as the
author of this work has been asserted by him in
accordance with the Copyright, Designs and Patent Act, 1988

Cover and book designed by Dickson Design

Printed by The Universities Press (Belfast) Ltd.

ISBN 0-9548998-0-6

Gordon Hannon

Acknowledgements

It would not have been possible to complete this book without the help assistance and encouragement of many people. Beginning closest to home I must first acknowledge the thought which began in the mind of my sister Ruth who originally came up with the proposal that Gordon Hannon's life deserved recognition in print. She also supplied her personal memories.

I owe a particular debt to my brothers Peter and Brian who accepted the constant responsibility of examining each section of the book as it came to life, and both of whom also provided much personal material. My other brothers, Leslie and Michael, from opposite ends of the family, supplied me with their individual memories. Peter was a mine of information about time spent in Africa. Brian kept me accurate on the subject of who was who in various Church of Ireland offices and also did helpful research on the history of the Trinity College Mission in Belfast. Michael established useful contacts in the TCD Library.

I am particularly grateful to Frank Taaffe who lives in Ardreigh, the old Hannon home in Athy, and who has been a wonderful source of the local history of the town, and to his wife Brige for her hospitality.

I must thank Cardinal Cahal Daly for giving me of his time and Rev. Bill Boyd who also provided information about the Churches' Industrial Council. David Bleakley, who was also a member of the Industrial Council, and his wife, Winnie, remembered details, particularly about experiences with Saidie Patterson.

Eric Turpin supplied invaluable memories of his time at TCD and Wolfhill and also provided a fascinating collection of photographs. Dr. Ken Stewart also remembered Wolfhill days. Thanks are due to Mrs Anne Evans who looks after Frank Buchman's U.K. archives and who took the trouble to search through them to find relevant material.

Mrs Helen Black (niece of Florrie Dowds) responded to my plea for help. Sammy Malcolm and Harold Hutchinson had fascinating memories of early days in Lurgan, where Wolsey Gracey, the Shankill Parish archivist, also gave great assistance.

In addition to those formally acknowledged within the text of the book, I must also thank Dr. Roddy Evans the author of 'The Breath of God' and George Daneel's Autobiography for additional African insights. Extracts from 'Saidie Patterson – Irish Peacemaker' by David Bleakley are printed by permission of Blackstaff Press.

Finally I would like to dedicate this book to the five wonderful women and one excellent man, each of whom was brave enough to take on the responsibility of marrying one of Gordon Hannon's children!

The Venerable Arthur Gordon Hannon M.A., Archdeacon of Dromore 1933-1939

Gordon Hannon

"I grew up with the object of being a Parson;
it never seriously occurred to me that God
had any other calling for me".

Gordon Hannon in 'Any Parson'

Introduction

In 1938, Archdeacon Gordon Hannon made the statement on the previous page. It was included in the draft of an unpublished book addressed to his fellow clergy, under the working title 'Any Parson'.

Made Canon at the age of 32 and Archdeacon of Dromore at 41, Gordon Hannon was on the steeply rising slope of a meteoric church career. Yet just two years after writing the book, at the age of 48, he stepped off the career ladder. What drove him to that decision? What inspired him?

How do you tell the story of a man's life? How do you see into his mind and soul, when you only knew him for the second half of his time on earth?

Beginnings

The story of the Hannon family in Athy, Co. Kildare begins with the arrival of John Hannon who came from Co. Limerick – the home country of the Hannon clan – around 1790.

John established a flour-milling business in the town which he ran and expanded during the rest of his 95 years. He was succeeded by his son Henry, who remained in charge until his death in 1888. In his turn, Henry was succeeded by John Alexander Hannon, the elder of twin sons and the father of Gordon.

John Alexander married Martha Rice and together they produced eight children: Reginald Richardson (Rex) (1889), Gladys (1890), Arthur Gordon (1891), John Coulson (known as Ion) (1893), Norman Leslie (1895), Marjorie (1896), Eileen (1900), and Ethel (1901).

When John took over the business, there were three mills operating, one in Athy, one in Castledermot and one at Ardreigh. Unfortunately John never had the same interest, drive or enthusiasm as his predecessors, and, in the face of competition from larger organisations, the undertaking began gradually to slip into decline. It is said that John actually had hoped to make a career in the church, but family pressures kept him involved in the business.

Most of their family were born while John and Martha lived near the mill at Castledermot, but after John's twin brother James died in 1897, they moved into the family house at Ardreigh, where the second mill stood on the banks of the canal.

Not far away, the River Barrow flowed past, and, in his early days, Gordon learnt the mysteries of fly-fishing along its banks; this was a passion which remained with him all his days, although other responsibilities seriously limited his opportunities. Of the four boys, Rex was always interested in farming and country pursuits; he was both a dashing horseman

From the top : Rex, Gladys, Gordon, Ion, Leslie, Marjorie, Eileen and Ethel.

Ready for golf with Ion c1907

The yard at Hannon's Mills, Athy, c1906

Gordon Hannon

Gordon's sporting caps - L-R : Corrig School 1stXV, Leinster Schools XV, and Trinity Athletics

Dublin University Athletics Team 1914. Gordon - Athlete standing back left

and a fine shot. Gordon, Ion and Leslie were more sports-minded, and achieved various degrees of success at rugby, on the running track and at the other social sports of the day. (Indeed, Gordon remained an aggressive and destructive croquet player whenever the opportunity arose. If ever there was a game invented to bring out the most un-Christian elements of a personality, it must be croquet!)

When the time came for school, Gordon was sent to stay with his mother's sister, Aunt Lilla Rice, who lived in Monkstown. From there he attended Corrig School in Kingstown. He was a tall lad – just over six foot – and, with some modesty, he used to say that it was only because he was much bigger than the rest of the school's First XV that he was invited to play for Leinster Schools against Ulster in March 1909. The Ulster Schools team was built around several star players who were destined to go on to appear on the international stage, so it is perhaps kindest to draw a veil over the result.

During his school years, Gordon was an active member of the Church of Ireland Young Men's Club and won prizes for Oratory and Essay–writing, both skills that would stand him in good stead as he developed them in his later ministry.

In holiday times, as he grew older, Gordon took an interest in the business where his father was struggling. Later, when he went to Trinity College Dublin, he used to spend some hours in the firm's Dublin office in the early morning, before going on to College for his full student day. This development of yet another skill helped to create the fully-rounded personality which he took with him into his studies in the Divinity School and, later in his life, into the Ministry of the Church.

At Trinity, Gordon worked hard and played hard – gaining some success at the mile and the half-mile on the athletics field. A much – treasured family possession is a dinner gong, suspended between a pair of horns, on a pedestal proudly bearing the inscription 'College Races 1910'.

With the problems in the family business, money was always fairly tight, but this proved a challenge in itself. Gordon used to describe how he hunted through the University handbook, seeking out details of prizes available in various abstruse subjects. On one occasion, he identified a £5 prize in Astronomy. With no special knowledge of the subject, he sought out the services of a crammer. The crammer's first instructions were 'Go and find out who is the examiner.'

When Gordon came back with the necessary information, he was told what the questions on the Prize paper would be. He went off and prepared answers based on the relevant text-books, and sure enough, when the paper was put in front of him, the predicted questions were there. The prize was his. Perhaps, indeed, he may even have been the only contestant; but £5 was not a sum to be ignored.

No one could say that Gordon Hannon was born with a silver spoon in his mouth. For all that, however, he certainly had been born into a golden age. Queen Victoria had celebrated her Gold and Diamond Jubilees. Great Britain had been at peace in Europe for half a century. Of course the 'Irish Problem' still rumbled on as Gladstone and his successors battled for a Home Rule Bill. But winters were crisp; summers were long. The Church of Ireland was flexing the strong Protestant muscles of its newly-acquired Disestablishment. All seemed very well with the world.

Gordon gained his B.A. in 1913, and in that same year was joined at TCD by his youngest brother Leslie, who began his degree studies as Gordon started on his two years in the Divinity School. In the sunny early summer days of Trinity Term 1914, the records show that Leslie finished 3rd in the Freshman's ½ mile, while Gordon finished 3rd in the 1 mile handicap.

But then came 4th August 1914, and, across the Continent, the great guns of Europe began to rumble.

The Trauma Years 1914 – 1916

Amid all the almost hysterical excitement of those autumn days in 1914, Leslie decided to break his University career and volunteered to join the Army. He was recruited into the King's (Liverpool Regiment), where he was commissioned as a 2nd Lieutenant.

Gordon was now entering his final year at Theological College. His first year of Divinity studies had won him the prestigious Archbishop King's Prize in 1914, and the Ecclesiastical History Prize followed in 1915. He was also awarded his Divinity Testimonium and was scheduled to be made Deacon at Whitsuntide in 1915.

All was going well. Pre-printed Field Service Post Cards arrived regularly from Leslie, who was at the Front in France. With all the possible unpleasant alternatives crossed out, one dated 5th May 1915 reads,

> *"I am quite well."*
> *"I have received your letter dated 2nd May 1915."*
> *"Letter follows **at first** opportunity."*
>
> Signature only   ***Les***

A short letter dated Saturday 8th May survives.

"Dear old Gordon,
Delighted to get your letter and hear of your splendid success. More power to your elbow! We are all well here – our rest is now at an end and off we go to-night – where I wonder?
    I suppose you got all my letters passed on and so get some news now and then! Weather glorious, heat terrible, but bathing good here.
    Best love and God bless you

Yours ever   *Les*

P.S. Remember me to all the lads."

Legacies of Leslie - Last postcard home, last letter home and memorial scroll with medals.

It was to be his last letter. On 16th May 1915, 2nd Lieutenant Norman Leslie Hannon was killed in action near Richbourg on the Western Front.

While all the family mourned, the preparations for Gordon's ordination had to move on, and by now he knew that his first job as a Curate would be in North Strand Parish, Drumcondra in Dublin.

Letters of sympathy on his loss included one from Mrs Selina Redding whose son Jack was one of Leslie's closest friends. A few months later, Gordon received a letter from Jack himself in which he describes going to find Leslie's grave and putting his own cross on it as he tidied it up. An indication of the horrors of the Front is reflected when he says *'It was a great relief to my mind to find it intact for I was afraid it might be hit with a heavy shell and blown to bits.'* He then goes on to quote a poem about Leslie, written by their Doctor.

"Staunch comrade, brave soldier, too soon fallen out,
I think of you stretched near the German redoubt,
With your blue Irish eyes gazing far into space
And the pallor of death on your fearless young face.
And I picture the night when our friendship was sworn,
When you stood up and sang us the Mountains of Mourne.

The hum of the bullets, the cannon's alarm
Still sound o'er the grave where you slumber so calm.
The wandering breezes at night time still moan
Round your grave, with wild flowers and grasses o'ergrown,
Far away from the loved ones who sorrow forlorn,
Far away from the beautiful Mountains of Mourne.

Life of course had to go on, and it was at about this time in 1915 that Gordon formed a remarkable friendship with Professor J.F. Gwynn, the Regius Professor of Divinity at Trinity, who at the age of 89 was living a life of semi-retirement, at his home in Clontarf.

Gordon had been appointed Auditor of the College Theological Society (the most senior student position), and must have made it his business to contact Professor Gwynn who was President of the Society. Fortunately for us, Dr. Gwynn was a prolific letter writer, and Gordon kept a collection of some 45 letters, written over the next two years, which have proved a valuable source of information about events unfolding in his life.

As Auditor of the 'Theo', Gordon was required to address the Society at its opening meeting of the 1915 – 16 academic year. His address on the subject of 'The War and Foreign Missions' was delivered on 8th November 1915, and was subsequently published by the University Press.

It was a major piece of work, and an analysis of its content shows that Gordon's mind had already grasped the concept of responsibilities for Christians far bigger and wider than the confines of the island of Ireland.

He describes the Great War as "the destruction of the edifice which men had reared in the name of Christianity. It was the downfall of that which, under the guise of Christianity, was being presented to the awakening peoples of Asia and Africa."

In Ireland, he says, "the masses were gradually turning their back on Christ. Materialism was quietly tightening its grasp on the nation. Men wondered why so many problems remained unsolved, when self-interest alone was striving to regulate the conduct of individuals and classes. Class was at war with class, creed with creed, and to human eyes it appeared next to impossible to avoid a civil war in the near future."

Later, he asks, "What then is the effect on the homeland? A fiery trial has been passing over us the last fifteen months. Suffering and sorrow have been knocking on every door." He continues, "The result of this fearful conflict must be a changed Europe, a changed Britain. If prosperity was the blessing of the old covenant, undoubtedly adversity is the blessing of the new. With faithful dependence on God, we may confidently believe that a changed Europe will mean a better, a regenerate Europe. Eyes are now open fact that the obstacles in the way of the advance of the Gospel of Christ were not so much the local problems of 'heathen' lands as our own lethargy at home, our fearful spiritual laxity."

Concentrating on the Missions, he says "The home country must be the key to the Mission field; a people at home, inspired by the impelling force of our triumphant, ascended Lord, would possess undreamt of powers for the furthering of Christ's Kingdom."

Later he speaks of contributions to the war from far away outposts of the Empire. "The loyalty of our Indian brethren, and their eagerness to help the Empire's cause, are magnificent. What return, then, is to be given for this wonderful patriotism, this loyalty of East to West? Their ambition is to be received into the brotherhood of nations. There could never be the same difficulties of colour and race when the war is over. It is un-Christian to deny that each in his own sphere is worthy of equal honour."

Towards the end of the address, he continues, "When Japan rejected Christianity her reason was that, judging from its effect on Western countries, it was not adequate to her needs. When that is grasped, and when the efforts of the Christian Church are understood as efforts to express an ideal, that ideal will never be described as inadequate to satisfy human needs."

Finally, he concludes, "Tremendous issues still hang in the balance: the greatest is the use we shall make of victory. The eyes of the Christian and the non-Christian nations of the world are focussed on us. Can we, will we, make it clear that our ambition is to win the world for Christ?"

Early in 1916, a letter from Dr Gwynn reveals that Gordon had become engaged to be married. At about the same time, another letter also reveals that Gordon had hoped to be ordained priest early, less than a year after being ordained deacon. He was evidently thinking of applying for service as an Army chaplain, so that he could feel that he was doing his duty, like both his younger brothers.

For by now Ion had also joined the Army and was in France with the 3rd Battalion of the King's (Liverpool) Regiment. Gordon kept many of his letters and Field Post Cards which date from early April 1916. In the event, Gordon's ordination to the priesthood eventually took place, as originally scheduled, on Trinity Sunday 18th June. Two days earlier, Dr Gwynn writes to him,

"You enter the Holy office of Priest, I know, in a humble spirit of self devotion and trust in the grace about to be given you to guide and strengthen you for its discharge. You have also, by nature – that is, by God's gift – abundant qualifications for the work.

"You must be conscious that you have in no common degree, the power of making friends and thus exerting influence. And you bring the blessing of an unstained manhood in the prime of youth and strength, in the dedication of yourself to the ministry of Christ's Church. 'Clean hands and a pure heart', a willing mind, zeal for God's service, grace to win and teach and guide His children in faith and obedience – and along with all these, a devout spirit constant in prayer.

"All these I know you have and I pray that you may be blessed and have guidance in the service of the gifts of nature and of grace which are yours to be used for the glory of the Giver.

I pray for you constantly."

By the time of his ordination, it appears that Gordon had, for the time being, put off any plans to try for Army chaplaincy.

Ion's dozen or more letters from France constantly show him in good spirits. At one time, he has been sent on a three-day course on how to deal with gas attacks. On his return, he has to give lectures to his men. He comments, "Hard at it today, lecturing on 'Anti-gas'. I have to go through the whole Battalion - 'Some Lecturer!' "

Legacies of Ion - Last letter home, uniform portrait and memorial scroll with medals.

The last letter is dated 2nd August, and the last Printed Field Post Card on 16th. Ion was killed two days later in that year's long Battle of the Somme.

In a letter at the end of the month, it is interesting to read Dr Gwynn writing to Gordon and saying, "I hope you don't hesitate to pray for the brothers who have been taken from you. Death has not put them beyond the reach of our prayers." A remarkable comment, in direct contradiction of Church of Ireland teaching at the time.

Gordon was able to spend the month of September at home with the family, and, for at least part of the time, he was joined by his fiancée. Other letters reveal only that her Christian name was Wynn, and that she was just about to start her 3rd year at T.C.D. Gordon was happily involved in coaching her in some of the subjects for the 'Littlego' examination, which comes at the beginning of that third year.

He has obviously written a good and descriptive letter to Dr. Gwynn, wondering, amongst other things, what is correct wear for a clergyman on holiday in the country. Dr. Gwynn writes "As to your outward get-up – What could be more appropriate! The white collar; the leggings – one end of you (the upper end) clerical, the other (lower) agricultural – and if his Grace the Archbishop should happen to visit, in making a round of the Diocese, and should remark on the composite attire, do just ask him if he never arrayed himself in the Vac with collar and black morning coat above, and his nether half in corduroy tights (relic of a former shooting party suit!). But I must stop with no more scandal against dignities."

A month later, Dr. Gwynn writes "Just a hasty line to congratulate you on your pupil's success in getting a 1st Class in Littlego. I wonder if the teacher would have been equally successful with a less interesting student – and the student to have learnt so well from a less devoted teacher!"

Early in December, Dr. Gwynn again writes in connection with Gordon's fiancée who has been listed as a speaker for the Elizabethan Society. "Perhaps as things advance, in times to come, a clergyman may be allowed to have pulpit help now and then from a wife who has had due training as a speaker."

Then, only three days later, he writes another letter - this time a letter of commiseration. He has just heard that Gordon's engagement has been broken off.

The final traumatic experience of the two traumatic years.

The Trinity Mission

During the period of Gordon's engagement to Wynn, she had made close friends with his sister Marjorie. Shortly after things came to an end, Marjorie sends Gordon a box of eggs with a little note enclosed saying, among other things, "I can't bring myself to believe that she has really ceased to love you."

In January 1917, Gordon returned home to Athy which awoke painful memories of happier times in September. He has obviously written of this to Dr. Gwynn who writes to him, in turn,

"I can well understand how your home visit brings back thoughts of your last holiday that must be very trying and full of regrets. Yet I dare say you can feel that after a break-off, the attempt to renew would be in vain and hardly practicable."

Suddenly, out of the blue, comes a letter from Dr. Newport White, the Professor of Biblical Greek and Archbishop King's Divinity Lecturer in Trinity College, Dublin, dated 27th January 1917.

"I am writing as President of the Belfast T.C.D. Mission to know if you would be willing to have your name submitted to the Committee as a candidate for the post of Head of the Mission.

".... The Head gets £100 and house and support; and as you may know, the financial position is always a source of anxiety. But the work is grand and has great possibilities; you are young, but that is all the better. This is a time for young men."

Gordon has been thinking about an opportunity for a second curacy – possibly in Waterford, where a new Dean has been appointed. He mentions this in a postcard acknowledgement of Dr. White's letter. A few days later, Dr. White writes again,

"I do not think that Waterford has any attractions except those of purely monetary nature.

"The position is this:- We of the Belfast Mission believe that you have qualities that would exactly suit the needs of the Mission. Many men, who would be just as acceptable as you are as curate of an ordinary parish would not suit the Mission at all. It is not a post that can be filled by anyone. This fact ought, I think, to weigh with you, without any false modesty."

Before continuing with Gordon's negotiations with the Committee, it is perhaps worth looking, briefly, at the background to the Mission

Founded in 1912, and based in buildings on Belfast's Shankill Road, the purpose of the Mission was to bring a meaningful presence of the Church of Ireland to the working class people of the area. Much of this would be based on pastoral visiting, getting to know the people and encouraging them to be prepared to join in worship at the Mission, without having to worry about being in their working clothes, or, for the women, being wrapped in their every-day shawls. There were organised activities to get boys off the streets. Most services were in the evenings on week-days. The first Head of the Mission was Rev. Arthur W. Barton (who later became Archbishop of Dublin and, coincidentally, confirmed three of Gordon's sons in the Chapel at St. Columba's College). Under his imaginative first leadership, activities included a Boys Club, a Bible Study group, a Savings Bank and attendances of as many as 250 including many 'shawlie' women at a series of Holy Week services.

The Mission had strong support from Bishop D'Arcy (Connor, Down and Dromore) who welcomed the T.C.D. students who would come up to help.

After Arthur Barton was moved by the Bishop to Dundela Parish in Belfast, the next Head was Rev. W. R. Manning. Problems continued over the lease of the Residence, (even Arthur Barton says he couldn't sort this out!). There was also the problem of raising money needed to meet the basic costs of salary and upkeep.

Following the letters from Dr. White, Gordon was now contacted by Dr. R.M. Gwynn, who confirms that the members of the Committee are anxious to know his position. At this time, Gordon received the last letter in his files from old Dr. Gwynn who strongly recommends him both to visit Belfast and see the Mission for himself and to contact Barton for more information. Gordon took that advice and kept draft copies of the letters he sent to R.M. Gwynn. He pulled no punches.

"It appears to me that, to fulfil its purpose, the Building itself wants a considerable amount of doing up. It presents anything but a T.C.D. air about it. Also, from what I saw and learned of the Mission, its objectives could not be attained unless there was an Assistant. The Head would want a certain amount of liberty to keep in touch with Trinity. If men were up at the Mission he would want to be free to attend to them.

"These things I state not wishing to criticise, but rather with a view to finding out if it is justifiable to ask any man to undertake an impossible task.

"I do not by any means want to shirk the work; if I undertook it I should put my whole weight into it, but at present it would only be possible to bury oneself in parochial work and leave almost all of the duties of a Head undone.

"While I was in Belfast, I came across several of the junior Clergy, and to put it plainly, they are disappointed with the Mission, and are quite decided that it could never be a success on the present lines. They look naturally for a centre of Trinity life to the Mission and they find no inducement to look a second time.

"I know there are great possibilities if run on the right lines – I know well the special difficulties of the time. You spoke of the value of the services to the Church and University – honestly I doubt this very much under the present conditions.

"Neither in the running of the Mission House itself, nor in the district, is there any Church atmosphere except under very forced circumstances, and although the people are proud to belong to 'Trinity College' – it's rather a shock to anyone to come from Trinity and see the building itself."

This letter shows an impressive self-confidence, especially when you remember that it is written by a young curate of less than 2 years of working experience, and was addressed to Dr R.M. Gwynn and Dr. Newport White, who were two of the key Church of Ireland figures among the powers that be in T.C.D.

Further letters from R.M. Gwynn and Gordon himself end in agreement on three basic matters,

1. That there should be an Assistant provided
2. That a sum of £30 be provided for urgent repairs and
3. That Gordon is not morally bound to remain for the normal term of office of three years.

With matters settled, Gordon is appointed, but is not released from his curacy by the Archbishop of Dublin until he has completed his two-year stint in North Strand.

On taking up office, Gordon is invited to attend meetings of the Committee. An appeal is launched in June 1917 and all outstanding debts are cleared by October. As the Mission is situated within the boundaries of St Mary's Parish, Gordon feels the need for a proper agreement with their Rector and Select Vestry. With Bishop D'Arcy's support, excellent relationships based on independence and interdependence are established between Parish and Mission and between Rector and Head of Mission.

When he arrived in Belfast, Gordon found himself faced with an interesting and tricky problem. Born and brought up in Co. Kildare, he had had no contact with the Orange Order. Now that he was living and working amongst the working class people of the Shankill Road – the very heartland of Ulster Protestantism, where the vast majority of the men were committed members of the Order – what should he do?

When he was invited to join Trinity Total Abstinence Loyal Orange Lodge Number 1282, he thought long and hard about his decision. He studied the Constitution of the Order and felt that he could accept the great majority of its written declarations of purpose. He also felt very strongly that accepting membership would help in the challenges faced by a young Southerner in identifying with the people.

Later in life, when he had moved to Lurgan, he realised most forcefully that the stresses laid by the Orange Order, locally, on the divisive elements of its purpose made it impossible for him to continue as a member, and he resigned. Whilst he could tolerate the concept of the defence of the Protestant Faith as a valid, positive attitude, he could not support what became, more and more obviously, the other side of the coin, which was often the denunciation of Roman Catholicism as a false, or even as an un-Christian way.

When he worked in Drumcondra in Dublin before coming to Belfast, Gordon had been heavily involved, as Curate, in running the Boys Brigade. Now in Belfast, he found that there was an existing organisation of Scouts. He realised that this was a useful recruiting mechanism for the youngsters of the area. St. Columba's College, Dublin and Portora Royal School, Enniskillen both supported these activities, with S.C.C. equipping the Boys Club Room and Portora hosting the summer camps. By the time Gordon eventually completed his service in the Mission, there was a Scout Troop, a Company of Girl Guides and there were two Packs of Wolf Cubs.

Talking retrospectively of those days, in a Radio Broadcast Appeal on behalf of the Mission, (some time in the 1930's), Gordon remembered the pride of the people when he said,

"There is no pauperisation, or indiscriminate giving of charity, which can so readily ruin self-respect. Even a recruit for the Wolf Cubs, though he may come along grubby and ill-clad, has to save, or earn, the price of his simple uniform. A real need is support for the Wolf Cub Camp – the one annual opportunity for 30 or 40 boys to see green fields, to bathe in sea and fresh air, and to revel in a complete change of environment."

Early in 1918, Gordon once again raises the question of being released to go to France as a Chaplain. R.M. Gwynn undertakes to write to him, pointing out the difficulties of the proposal and also pointing out the need for caution in pursuing the request, in view of Bishop D'Arcy's attitude to the idea.

After the Armistice in November 1918, Gordon raises the possibility of getting help from ladies, possibly forming a Ladies Auxiliary. He suggests the idea of an informal approach to women students. (Note: Men students have regularly given help from time to time.) In 1919 a Ladies Auxiliary is formed.

Council records show that the Mission is in a much healthier condition. The Hon. Treasurer decides to take a more aggressive policy. More publicity about the work and objects of the Mission is launched in T.C.D. itself. Gordon is authorised to hold a public meeting in Belfast and to prepare an illustrated appeal for circulation to Trinity graduates.

Plans are launched to develop a new site for the Mission. The Rector of St Mary's gives his full support. With backing from Bishop D'Arcy, the salary of the Head's Assistant is now to be paid by Belfast's 'Additional Clergy Fund'. By October 1919, an estimate of £2,100 for constructing a new building is accepted, and a sub-committee arranges a Bank loan with the Belfast Bank. Dr. Newport White, Dr R.M. Gwynn and Dr. McNeill who are on the Committee agree to act as guarantors of the loan. The other members decline!

In 1920, Gordon is re-appointed for a second 3-year term. He has himself appointed the Rev. Charles Lyndon as his Assistant. The Committee agree terms with Mr. Lyndon that he should take over as Head should Gordon take up another position during the second three-year appointment. In October 1920, the new Hall has been built. On November 18th Gordon writes to the Secretary of the Committee to inform them of his appointment to Ballymoney Parish as Rector. The Institution date is fixed for 16th December. His letter continues.

"My thanks to the Committee for a wonderfully happy three years and eight months. It is a joy to me that you all seem pleased with my efforts. There is great work to be done for God now, and I hope the new Head will get every support."

While formal correspondence follows, it is perhaps worth quoting the following personal letter from Dr. Newport White.

"My Dear Hannon,

Your Postcard announcing your appointment to B----y has reached me this evening too late for immediate reply. It was not unexpected; yet the definite act, the declaration of fait accompli, has something of the effect of a big clock striking twelve in a silent night.

Nothing remains but to express again my warm appreciation of what you have done for the T.C.D. Mission in Belfast, to express an earnest hope – a confident anticipation – for your success in the future, and a somewhat anxious thought for the future of our Mission without you.

I wish it had been possible for the change to have taken place a little later. At the same time I have a high opinion of Lyndon, and I believe, now that the Hall is actually built, that the people have grit enough to keep it going.

I should like, here, to say how much I feel we are indebted to you for the friendly, brotherly feeling which I perceive in Mr Browne's* attitude towards the Mission. I notice a great change in his demeanour and action, and I am sure that it is greatly due to your tact and gentlemanly Christianity. There is a Christianity – quite real – that is un-gentlemanly.
Believe me, with kindest regards and the best of good wishes,

Yours very sincerely

N.J.D. White"

* The Rector of St Mary's Parish

A formal Resolution is passed by the Committee:

"That the members of the Executive Committee of the T.C.D. Mission in Belfast desire to place on record their sincere appreciation of the magnificent work carried out by Rev. Gordon Hannon while Head of the Mission during the last 3 years. The work was carried out by Mr. Hannon at a time of great stress and difficulty, and it was carried out by him with unfailing faith and courage, and thanks to his great exertions a Mission building has been provided. And to their great regret he now resigns his post, leaving a sphere of great possibilities to his successor . . . . Mr. Hannon was appointed a Vice-President of the Mission."

Bishop D'Arcy writes to the Secretary:

"I was really very sorry to move Mr. Hannon, but the necessities of The Church demanded it. How wonderfully he has been blessed in the Mission and I think that not the least of his ability is to be shown in his having left all in a position to continue and develop after him."

Finally, in this chapter, the Report of the General Committee for 1920 includes,

"The Mission has lost in the person of the Rev. A. Gordon Hannon, a very devoted Head, an able organiser, and an untiring worker for the cause. The people of Belfast have rallied round Mr Hannon in magnificent fashion in raising much of the funds needed to erect the Mission Hall. They have given generously and by far the largest portion of the money collected for the building has been subscribed in Belfast. The people of the district also have given of their best and their subscriptions towards the upkeep of the Hall are increasing in a wonderful way."

And so to North Antrim and the market town of Ballymoney.

Ballymoney

When Gordon moved to Ballymoney as Rector, Marjorie, the oldest of his three younger sisters, came with him to act as his housekeeper. The fact that he only stayed in the Parish for three years, while learning and practising the exercise of the duties of a Rector, suggests that he learnt quickly and soon mastered the practicalities of what was involved.

However, in the story of his life, present and future, these three years were in many ways to be the most momentous of all. For it was during this time that he met and married Hilda Denny.

What follows now is taken from her own memoirs, which she put on paper around 1989.

The 'I' telling the story is of course Hilda herself.

'When I was about seventeen, a new bachelor Rector came to Ballymoney about 9 miles away. He had an unmarried younger sister who kept house for him, and I may tell you there was a great fluttering in the dovecotes of the County when they realised that this young man had arrived among us, very charming and good looking, from a good family background in the South.

'My sister, Cis, met him before I did at a dance which I was not considered old enough to attend. However, during the Easter holidays before my last term at school there was a 'thé dansant', a very popular form of afternoon dance held at Leslie Hill, the big house of Ballymoney, and there Gordon and I met.

'It really was a case of 'love at first sight'. As I had my hair up which was compulsory at school if you were a prefect, my darling man must have thought I was older than I was. We danced nearly all the time together and when I was going home on the back of a motorbike that one of my boyfriends had brought me on, he kept muttering about "that bloody parson" and nearly threw me off! – My friends were nearly all boys and young men and we had hilarious times together. I learnt one very salutary lesson from some of their conversations when they forgot I was there. For instance, in referring to one particular girl I heard one of them say "Och her; you could have her for sixpence". I vowed then, "You'll never have the chance of saying that about me, my lad!" I think that this was probably the main thing that kept me on the straight and narrow in those days of the early 1920's when so many of the young were growing up in a heady atmosphere of the 'bright young things' and had every chance of going astray.

'I went back to school for my final term and we didn't meet again until a great picnic which was held annually at White Park Bay in August for my cousin Alan Traill's birthday. Great preparations were made for this. A donkey cart set off at screech of dawn laden with peats for the fire, pots of potatoes, lots of cold chicken and ham and gorgeous grapes from the Ballylough green houses. There were usually about 30 or 40 people at this picnic including a great friend of mine, Captain Alex Cramsie of O'Harabrook, who happened to be one of Gordon's leading parishioners. I used to ride and hunt ponies for him when they were still a bit much for his three young sons. Apparently at some point of the day Alex said to Gordon, indicating me, "There's a wee girl who would do you nicely, Hannon." To which 'Hannon' replied "I think you've got very good taste!"

'A great 'Coming Out' Ball was planned for me on 16th September, shortly before my 18th birthday. I was very excited as I had my first proper evening dress. I remember it well: pale green chiffon with trailing pink rosebuds with their leaves. This was in the day of 'programmes' and when Gordon arrived, all 6'1" of him, looking absolutely superb in white tie and tails, my heart turned about six somersaults. He scribbled his name over most of my programme including the supper dance. The ballroom was full and, of course, everyone was watching us dancing so much together – rather to my mother's dismay.

'One of the great moments of my life came when we 'sat out' two dances together on a balcony of the house with a perfect full harvest moon shining down on us. We stood gazing at it for a while and then suddenly he took me in his arms and kissed me good and proper! He was nearly a foot taller than me and I was completely engulfed in that wonderful embrace. I can still at the age of 76 feel the thrill of that moment. Presently we sat down and, taking one of the rosebuds off my frock, he said in his deep wonderful voice, "Darling, I'm going to ask you to marry me, but not yet." Shaken to the core, we returned to the ballroom and managed to behave with due propriety.

'Our next meeting was at the Boxing Day meet of the Route Hunt which was always held at Beardiville House where my Uncle Hugh Leckie lived. A few nights later at another dance he did propose to me while we sat out on the stairs with a rather drunken fellow walking up and down over us. I said "Yes, with all my heart." As chaperones were the order of the day, my father was playing bridge with the rest of the chaperones (my poor mother was in bed with the 'flu). When he got home, Dad said to her, "Hannon is coming to see me in the morning about Hilda" to which my mother replied, "Good Lord! Is the man mad? Does he know what he's doing?"

The following day arrived and after talking with my father the pair of them went up to see my mother who was still in bed. She welcomed Gordon charmingly but added once more "Do you know what you are taking on? You'll probably find her hanging by her heels from the church steeple!" Gordon laughed, "Surely I'll take her on; there's great stuff in her and I love her so very much!" (He told me all this afterwards.)

'After much consultation, my parents agreed to a public engagement on the basis that it must be for a full year as I was so young, and we had to be content with that.

'Shortly after that, Gordon had a fortnight's holiday and we planned to go down South to meet his people. At that time the Civil War was in full swing and it was often quite an undertaking to get from North to South and vice versa. However, when we arrived in Belfast we were told that an armoured engine with two carriages was going to try to get through to Dublin. Apart from very gingerly crossing some half blown-up bridges and waiting for a reported ambush to be cleared, the train duly arrived at Amiens Street station in Dublin to a great welcome.

'Another sister of Gordon's met us with a funny old bull-nosed Morris car and we drove the fifty miles without incident to Athy near where Gordon's home was. I was feeling rather nervous at the thought of meeting my future in-laws, but indeed I needn't have been for their welcome was so warm and their hearts wide open to me. Gordon's mother was such a warm motherly person with a terrific sense of humour. His father was a charming gentle old man with failing eyesight and an air of sadness about him. He had lost his two youngest sons in the war.

'During the fortnight we were there we were royally entertained all over the counties of Kildare and Carlow. I had two wonderful hunts on a point-to-point thoroughbred winner belonging to Rex, Gordon's elder brother.

'At that time our love for each other grew more deep and passionate, and I often thank God that I had a man with enough decency and moral courage for us both – for indeed I wouldn't have minded what we had done! Isn't that a terrible confession from a grandmother of nearly 77!

'During the early summer of our engagement year we were invited to Scotland to stay with my Denny relations who were all agog to see what kind of brave man (especially a clergyman!) could possibly have the courage – or foolhardiness – to want to marry *me*!'

Hilda goes on to describe how a big wedding was planned for April 11th 1923. Everything was going wonderfully smoothly when, out of the blue, tragedy struck. The news came from Athy that Gordon's father had died. For years he had been suffering from depression following the loss of the two boys, his own failing eyesight, and the problems with the business. Efforts had been made to try to keep his shotgun safely away from him, but he must have been determined to end his life.

Hilda picks up the story again,

'My mother-in-law to be was staying with us for the wedding and, of course, she and Gordon had to go straight away to the funeral. Before they left, we all decided that it would be best to go on with the wedding, but cancel the reception and just have the bridal party and a few old friends to

Bride and Groom leaving Billy Parish Church

Hilda's brother Jim piping them out

The Bridal Party

lunch beforehand. The Primate, Dr. D'Arcy, together with Gordon's uncle, Rev. James Henry Rice, took the service beautifully.

'How my poor husband survived the first year or two of my cooking efforts I will never know, but he was so loving and encouraging that before long I learned how to be a reasonable housekeeper and a good cook. One of the unfortunate things about being brought up with an army of servants was that I could hardly even make a cup of tea, nor had I learnt how to do any washing! As a helper I had a young girl, Sarah, aged 15 and quite untrained, so the pair of us often made a hash of things.

'Almost immediately I found I was pregnant and my parents insisted that as I was so young I should be under the care of a Belfast specialist, Tommy Holmes, and have the baby in his private nursing home.

'Gordon used to take me out on long brisk walks every evening, wet or shine, and I never felt better in my life. The baby was due in February, but one evening, on December 31st, I began to feel rather queer. Gordon had gone out to a series of meetings to finish up with the Watch Night service in the Church at the bottom of our avenue. By 9.00 pm Sarah was due to go home as she didn't sleep in, but I asked her to stay the night and she readily agreed to do so. I went to bed with hot bottles to try to get rid of the gripping pains in my tummy. Imagine such ignorance! About 10.00 I said to Sarah "I think you had better go and find a doctor, any doctor, for I think I'm going to die." Off she went and didn't come back for an hour. But she had found a doctor who examined me and said "Oh yes, we'll have a little stranger here any time now." "But Doctor," I wailed, "It's not due for over a month!" He asked where my nurse was, and when I told him I hadn't got one and was supposed to be in Belfast, he just laughed and went off and returned eventually with a very nice woman who was a retired maternity nurse.

'Sarah went off to try to find Gordon. She got him just as he was going into church to start the service before midnight. He hastily re-arranged the service so that he preached at the beginning and then left the rest to the Curate. Then he tore up the avenue, cassock and surplice flying, and arrived just in time to hear the lusty yells of his firstborn son. Leslie, as we called him, was over a month premature, but although only 6lbs was very strong and healthy. We both wondered what some of the old pussycats in the Parish thought of our dates! However everyone was delighted and we received many congratulations.

'Leslie was to be the only one of our family to be born in Ballymoney for when he was just a year old, Gordon was appointed Rector of Lurgan Parish.'

Lurgan 1924 - 1940

Arrival

Gordon's appointment as Rector of Lurgan Parish in 1924, represented an extraordinary leap forward in his career, combined with a considerable act of faith by those who made the appointment.

Consider for a moment his C.V. to that date;
Age: 32
Curate as Deacon and then Priest, Drumcondra 1915-1917
Head of T.C.D. Mission, Belfast 1917-1920
Rector Ballymoney 1920-1923

And now appointed Rector of what was possibly the largest Parish, in Church of Ireland population terms, in the whole country. Remarkably, more than half of the population of the town were members of the C. of I. – over 6000 parishioners in all.

Awaiting Gordon's arrival were three curates, all of whom elected to stay on and work with the new Rector. One of them, Rev. J.T. Belton, later Rector of Kilkeel, was himself 5 years older than Gordon.

When Bishop Grierson, Bishop of Down, Connor and Dromore, writes to Gordon to tell him the decision of the Board of Nomination, he makes no bones about the challenge ahead.

> "I know that this has come to you apart from yourself. Thus you can feel that it is indeed God's call to you. There is I believe no finer post in the Church of Ireland; - that is if great opportunities for Service amongst a local mass of Church folk constitutes such a post. But I feel quite sure that under God's blessing you will rise to it.
>
> I know you so well (at least I think I do!) that I will not now say much to you as regards your need of closeness of life with Him who is our life. That I am sure you realise. You have already found, I am sure, that in the suppression of self, and in calmness of

trust, true wisdom is given.
As I said to you the other day, there may be difficulties at first –
but the vast majority will rally round you and uphold your
decisions when they see strength and God–given wisdom in your
decisions. The flock are yearning for a leader and God will enable
you to be that.
I informed the Board of Nomination that to show my thorough
agreement with the appointment and also to show my sense of the
importance of the Parish, I intended, when you were instituted, to
offer you the Canonry vacant by Dean Clarendon's appointment
and I hope you will accept this."

Many others wrote at the same time with a remarkable variety of
comments.

Archbishop D'Arcy writes from Armagh 'You will find that the
Lurgan people will respond to every effort you make for them. They are the
same stock that we have here – people who love their Church and are ready
to make great sacrifices for her.'

Dr. Newport White writes from Dublin 'You are going to Lurgan with
the approval of your bishop, as is evidenced by his addition of the Canonry
to you. Personally, I cannot help an unworthy feeling of pleasure in having
got you up into the North in the first place.'

Gordon's mother writes 'Just a hurried line to let you know how proud
and pleased we are. Fancy, my son a Canon. Now mind I have £50 available
any time you would like a loan.'

G.A. Chamberlain, Rector of the Mariner's Church in Kingstown
writes: 'Your task will be a heavy one, as I fear the Church is in a somewhat
derelict condition, but you are fortunate in going there at an age when hard
work is both possible and a pleasure.'

Arthur Barton writes a long letter which says in part 'Being an
unsuccessful candidate but by no means a disappointed one I want to be

among the first to offer you my very best good wishes in connection with Lurgan! I was honestly delighted to hear the result because I did not think that they had the sense to appoint a man like you. I think you are the very man for the job. It's a great adventure – an adventure for God, and I thank God that they have appointed a strong man.

If I may, as an old friend, venture to give one piece of practical advice (for your wife's sake) – Be sure that they thoroughly overhaul the Rectory before you go in. They are always much more willing to do things like that *before* one goes in than *after*. They ought to paper and paint it from top to bottom, and *thoroughly test the Drains*.'

Parish Life

When Gordon arrived in Lurgan with his young wife and their one-year-old son, he found himself in a totally new situation with a variety of fresh challenges.

In terms of 'churchmanship', Shankill Parish in the early 1920's was very much at the 'low' end of the spectrum. The building itself, as his friend Chamberlain had suggested, was not in great repair. It was enormous, with a designed capacity for around 1800 people, but which could hold some 2000 at a crush. Everything in the building was plain, with only the most minimal decorative features. The clergy wore only long white albs, with no cassocks – a style of dress to which Gordon was not accustomed.

Hilda describes the situation in her memoirs:

'When we went to Lurgan first, Gordon was warned that there was quite a crowd of rather narrow-minded people who highly disapproved of anything they felt smacked of 'Popery'! One thing was their dislike of the wearing of cassocks, with the result that the clergy all wore long white surplices which looked like nightgowns. When Gordon said that cassocks and academic hoods must be worn and surplices be a decent length, I remember the curates all being highly nervous about what would happen. However, on the first Sunday they all trooped in properly attired and one of the principal objectors said later, "The new Rector is a fine fellow, and I don't care if he comes in in his pyjamas!" '

Hilda continues, 'Another stumbling block was the firm refusal of the congregation to stand while the clergy were processing in. Gordon quietly got rid of this by announcing the first hymn from the Vestry door so everyone had to get up and were all singing lustily by the time the clergy came in.'

Hilda herself caused quite a stir. 90-year-old Harold Hutchinson, still going strong in 2003, remembers the milkman who called at the Rectory to take the order for future requirements, and began flirting with the pretty girl who answered the door. It was only when the girl failed to turn up for the date he had made, that the milkman discovered that he had been chatting up the new Rector's wife.

As we have already seen from his days at the Trinity Mission in Belfast, Gordon was an enthusiastic supporter of the Boy Scouts organisation. It is perhaps hard to realise just how new an idea this was at the time; Baden-Powell had only founded it in 1908. Gordon soon realised that it would be very useful to have a Troop in Lurgan and First Lurgan was founded in 1925. The idea was an immediate success, and, any time you talk to people about the Lurgan days, one of the first things they mention is the Scouts.

There were more than just the one Troop formed over the years, and each summer, Gordon would take eighty or ninety youngsters to the Isle of Man, or to Scotland, for the annual camp. Harold Hutchinson, one of the original recruits, remembers a visit to Scotland, where the camp was led by Gordon and Rev. George Bulger, one of the curates. When sea-bathing, Gordon was anxious about the boys' swimming ability. He walked out from the beach to waist depth, and announced that no-one should go any deeper. However, George Bulger had other ideas, or maybe he just didn't hear the instruction. He grabbed Harold and dumped him in the sea a bit further out.

Harold described what happened next. 'I couldn't swim and I went down for the first time and then for the second time. Just then the Rector turned round and saw what was happening. He reached out and grabbed me by the hair and pulled me out. Then he turned on Mr Bulger. He was raging. "Do you not realise you might have made that lad frightened of the water for the rest of his life?" I never saw him so angry before or since.'

The new chancel - note the 'upside-down' crosses in the wall panels

Gordon with a group of his senior Scouts c1930

Gordon Hannon

After about five years in the Parish, Gordon thought that the time had come to do something about the Church itself, and a great plan was started on a complete re-design of the Sanctuary. The entire structure was to be made in Carrera marble, and the design for the lower wall behind the Communion Table was a series of rectangular shapes below a frieze. The whole thing had to be imported from Italy, and obviously had to be made up of a large number of small segments. Unfortunately, the divisions into sections were made right down the middle of each of the rectangles, which meant that each piece was quite clearly to be seen as the shape of a cross. At that time, the Church's regulations were very specific about the placing of any representation of the Cross above or behind the Holy Table. When all the beautiful slabs of polished marble arrived and were seen stacked outside the building, a great rumpus blew up.

The question was 'What could be done?' The work had been completed in accordance with the design, so there was no way it could be rejected. The costs involved were well in excess of £2,000 – an enormous sum at the time. Then inspiration struck. Gordon decided that the problem would be solved if the whole of the frieze was installed exactly as designed – but upside-down! This proved totally acceptable to all, and to this day the decoration of the Sanctuary in the church looks just as it did when it was finally completed in 1932.

In December of that same year, Gordon received a letter from Bishop Grierson offering, and inviting him to accept, the position of Archdeacon of Dromore which was due to fall vacant early in 1933. The letter reads in part-

> 'It gives me great pleasure to do this for your long faithful
> service to our Church, in the Diocese, & especially in Lurgan,
> which has been so long and consistently successful – indeed merits
> recognition.
> To my Archdeacons I frequently turn for help – and that help I feel
> sure you will loyally grant me.
> That God's blessing may ever rest on you and yours is the earnest
> prayer of
> Your sincere friend,
> Charles T P Down'

Throughout his life, in any new Parish, Gordon always made it one of his first priorities to establish positive contact with the local Parish Priest, and in Lurgan he had very quickly made friends with Canon O'Hagan. On at least one occasion this good relationship paid dividends in the town.

There was always considerable tension between the two communities and, as the marching season approached, trouble was often not far beneath the surface. On one particular day, Gordon had been to Belfast for a Diocesan Council meeting, and, as was the custom in those days, was wearing his full archidiaconal uniform with frock coat and gaiters. When he got home, the telephone was ringing. It was an agitated Canon O'Hagan calling to say that a riotous mob was heading for the Portadown Road where many Catholics lived. Could Gordon help?

Immediately, without bothering to change his outfit, Gordon jumped back into the car, and drove up the town where he found the mob following a large, rather drunken man waving a huge Union Jack on a long pole. Gordon grabbed the pole and shouted, 'Come on lads. Follow me!' With the skirts of his frock coat flying as he danced along, he led the crowd back up the town, right away from potential trouble. On that occasion at least, the day was saved.

Congregations throughout Gordon's rectorship were huge, particularly by modern standards. A spot check showed an average figure of around 750 worshippers at Morning Prayer, with a maximum figure spotted of 1095, and an average of over 1000 for Evening Prayer, again with a maximum of 1675. These evening services were very popular with the younger parishioners. Harold Hutchinson said, "The services were at 7.30. and if you didn't get a seat up in the Gallery by 7 o'clock, you would have to sit with the older folk downstairs."

Gordon really enjoyed those evenings. He loved the sound of good congregational singing, and although there was a good big Choir of some 60 voices, he used to come out into the church at around 10 past 7, wearing his cassock, and have a good session of hymn practice with the congregation, before the service began.

Florrie Dowds, whom we will meet later in this chapter, remembers one occasion which illustrates the discipline and respect Gordon brought to his position.

She was at the evening service with some friends, and they were chattering to each other when Gordon went to read the lesson. The church fell silent except for Florrie and her friend. Gordon stood still at the Lectern, looking up towards the gallery. The silence grew more intense, until Florrie and her companion suddenly realised that everyone was looking at them. "Have you finished your conversation?" asked Gordon. Silence. "Well if you're ready, I'll begin." How they wished the floor would open!

The minutes of the General Easter Vestry of 1937 quote from Gordon's address to the meeting. "I have a feeling, as a Rector of a parish like Shankill, that I have a very special job to do. It is my job to be able to train people to take spiritual responsibility, to see what God is demanding in their own lives.

"I feel that my job is dealing with the kind of men I see here before me, of sitting down with them, and together finding out how they and I should embark on the next step to be taken for God; how together we could each of us get the powers within us more and more released for the Kingdom of God."

Family Life

The Rectory in Lurgan must have been one of the ugliest houses of its type in Ireland! It was a big square lump with only two redeeming features. The first was a pleasantly designed rose window above the front door. The second was that the house was big enough. It is worth remembering that Gordon was the father of a growing and a 'growing-up' family.

In addition to Leslie, Peter was born in 1927, I (David) was born in 1930 and Ruth, as a wonderful birthday present for Gordon, on April 16th, in 1932. During our early years, the regular staff in the Rectory consisted of a Nurse, a Cook and a Housemaid, all of whom lived in.

Beginning in 1930, a series of very unpleasant illnesses hit the family. Peter caught diphtheria, which was a really frightening disease at that time. Fortunately, he came through it, without any of the other children being infected.

Next, in 1931, I myself had a mysterious and very poisonous infection (many years later identified to me as osteomyelitis), in the elbow of my right arm. At first, the doctors felt that the only possible treatment was to amputate the arm. Hilda fought with them to think again. They then came up with the suggestion of amputation at the elbow itself. Hilda didn't think that was much of an improvement! She still argued until, eventually, the doctors agreed to try an experimental treatment which involved opening up the joint and putting in a drain, in the hope of getting rid of the poison, all with no guarantee of success. The arm would then have to be set permanently, either in a straight position, or bent at a right-angle. Hilda accepted this idea, and settled for the right-angled solution.

The situation was genuinely a matter of life and death, and Hilda used to describe the scene in the waiting room at the hospital. She, herself, marching up and down the room swearing like a trooper, while Gordon knelt, praying quietly, in the corner. Her courage in fighting with the doctors was rewarded when the operation was a total success and I woke up from the anaesthetic, looked at her, and said quite clearly, "Bottle!". While I recovered from the operation, Hilda used to exercise the arm as I was feeding, with the result that I have had almost total freedom of movement and use of it, all my life.

Apart from general family infections, with all the usual childhood afflictions such as chicken-pox, whooping cough, or mumps turning the Nursery into a miniature hospital ward, there were no further major health dramas until 1934.

Then, as if the problems with my arm had not been serious enough, the next major challenge arose when Peter contracted Polio. The treatment at the time involved lying flat for at least six months, to try to stop the disease from spreading to other parts of the body. Peter had lost the use of the calf muscle and the Achilles tendon of his right leg, and, once he was allowed to try to move about, he had to wear a heavy calliper boot, with straps to hold metal supports to his leg.

Luckily for him, and for the whole family, it was recommended that he should be taken to a talented young osteopath called Ted Dunham, who had just returned from training in America. Ted's first instruction was that the dreaded boot would have to be got rid of, if Peter was to have the chance of becoming reasonably mobile. Ted also recommended taking Peter to be examined by a brilliant paediatric surgeon, who was the only man trying out experimental surgery to treat this condition. By good fortune he was working in Liverpool at the Children's Hospital.

In a major operation, the muscular structure of Peter's damaged leg was repaired by the transfer of muscle elements which exist in other people, but are effectively dormant. This revolutionary treatment resulted in Peter being able to play most sports (even including Rugby up to the age of 13), and he went on to play cricket and tennis for St.Columba's, and, later, even squash for Keble. He played good golf, to a single figure handicap, and became an energetic cyclist, developing particularly powerful muscles in his 'good' leg.

This detailed story of Peter's development was particularly worth telling because it reflects Gordon and Hilda's determination to keep life as normal as possible for all of us children.

All these traumatic events were taking place before, around, and after, the time in 1932 when Gordon became involved with the Oxford Group. As will become evident in the next chapter, it can be safely said that these were not the easiest years in his married life.

Both Gordon and Hilda were keen games players. Hilda, particularly, continued to play top class competitive hockey - an activity consistently interrupted by the bearing of children until Brian was born in 1936. After that she took up golf, quickly reaching the more than respectable level of a 16 handicap.

In the summertimes, Gordon and Hilda both played competitive tennis for Windsor Tennis club in Lurgan, and of course Gordon tried to keep himself fit throughout the year, with good golf and occasional forays onto the hockey field. The story is told of him making his first appearance for Belfast YMCA, when he was 39 years old, and had been a Canon for some seven years. The Belfast Telegraph's Sports special 'Ireland's Saturday Night' carried the interesting comment, "The new man on the left wing is a likely looking lad, very fast, and should do well with a little more experience."

We were all encouraged to take part in games from our early days – indeed we invented many of our own, often involving highly dangerous 'Rectory bikes' which were bought second-hand, and usually had few of the generally-considered necessary elements such as good brakes. What the good people of Lurgan thought when they saw Peter and me on a Sunday evening, no longer in our Sunday best but back in our everyday clothes, out on our bicycles, riding round and round the Salvation Army Band, as it made its way up the town, is hard to imagine.

Gordon and Hilda must have had great patience, for I certainly don't remember times when we were not involved on the golf course. When the great Fred Daly (Ireland's only Open Golf Champion) came to Lurgan Golf Club as a young professional, he made special cut down wooden-shafted clubs for us, so that we could start as soon as we were interested. Because Leslie was not particularly keen on either golf or tennis, it became quite normal, as we were growing up, that Gordon and I would play against Hilda and Peter. These partnerships indulged in many hard-fought battles over the years. Tantrums were not tolerated!

In the family play-room, I must confess that things were not always quite so well regulated! All games, whether board games (Snakes and Ladders, Ludo, etc.), or card games of all sorts (Old Maid, Snap or Beggar-my-Neighbour), were played with both Leslie and, later, Ruth, also involved.

I am told that I had a short fuse to my temper (what a ridiculous idea!!), and there is little doubt that Peter took considerable delight from setting light to it.

In the 1930's, it was quite a normal practice to run an account in shops where you were a regular customer, and, when we went shopping with her, we would often hear Hilda say, "Would you put that on the Rectory account". This seemed a very efficient method of shopping, without having to produce cash! In the summer of 1936, when I was attending Lurgan Model Public Elementary School, I adopted the technique myself. Walking home from school, we passed an ice-cream shop. One day I marched in and had a 'penny poke' (an ice-cream cone). "Put it on the Rectory account." I announced. There was no problem, so I repeated the practice each day.

Eventually, the end of the month arrived and a small brown envelope turned up in the post. 'The Account' had arrived. To someone whose 'Saturday Money' was three pence, a total amount of nearly two shillings (24 pence) was huge. I'm not sure how Gordon managed to keep a straight face, but he did, and I learnt that there was such a thing as fiscal rectitude! My pocket money was reduced to little more than the bare essential of a penny for the collection plate in Church.

In 1936, Brian was born and, by that time, the four older children were old enough for there to no longer be a need for a Nurse for them. Gordon and Hilda recruited Florrie Dowds, mentioned earlier, specifically to look after the new baby. With her arrival, someone very, very special became part of the family. Florrie herself was the third youngest member of a large Lurgan family, with 4 brothers and 7 sisters, so, although her original responsibilities were specially for Brian, she had no problem in dealing with the rest of us, as and when the need arose.

Later in life, as we grew up, Florrie often kept the household running when Gordon and Hilda were travelling, and she provided much wise counsel to all of us at various times, in our own difficulties – great and small. She shared many of our secrets, she dried many of our tears, and she enjoyed many of our pleasures, through the course of the next 25 years.

Leslie, writing from America, has his own memories. He writes "I always remember Pop in the late 20's/early 30's, sitting in his study in the Rectory on Saturday mornings, working hard on his sermon, with his pipe going strong – clouds of blue smoke. He finally quit later.

1931 Gordon (with pipe!) Leslie and Peter

1933 Gordon (no pipe!) David, Ruth and Peter

1932 Hilda ready for Lough Neagh with Peter behind, David in front and Leslie 'independant'

Gordon Hannon

"He was illustrating his sermon one time, talking about a rather lovely beaten-brass tray, (a favourite of Mama's which we cherish now), which he kept referring to as our 'battered-brass' tray. It was a long time before Mama stopped teasing him about it! At the same time, he specially enjoyed listening to the cricket test matches on the old wireless we had. I would have fun 'helping' him to tune the double tuner dials to get decent reception – he never could quite understand that, at that time, you had to balance the input and output sides of the set to make it work. The speaker was a large horn that sat on top of the set. My job on Saturday mornings was to remember to take the 2-Volt wet battery to the shop to swap it for the re-charged one.

"Towards the end of our stay in Lurgan, I was very interested in buying an old motorbike – an ancient 500cc Norton that had been used for racing. Since Pop had ridden motorcycles in his younger days (courting Mama from Ballymoney), he insisted on giving it a test ride. With straight-through exhaust and no silencer, the noise was horrendous, and our Kerry Blue dog, Darkie, went ballistic, chased him down the avenue, and bit him firmly in the leg! Goodbye bike!!

"Pop loved working in the greenhouse – pollinating and pruning grapes and peaches, and growing tomatoes – he was very good at these. He and Hugh Clarke (our gardener, cow milker and general factotum) would have long, detailed discussions about what to do next. The rest of the large kitchen and flower garden was Mama's domain.

"Ma and Pa played quite a lot of mixed hockey. My memories, as a kid watching them, are that it was a pretty vicious 'game', with no holds barred – the men playing somewhat gentlemanly and the women taking advantage of that.

"One sad thing I remember Ma telling me about. Pop was called out late one dark night to visit someone out in the country. He was driving quite slowly in miserable weather, went round a corner, and the next thing he knew, there was a horrendous bump and a man lying dead on the bonnet of the car. The poor man had been riding his bicycle with no lights or reflectors, wearing typical dark country clothes, and was virtually invisible. Pop was totally exonerated of any fault, but Ma told me that he suffered dreadfully from nightmares for several years, and ever after, tried, where possible, to avoid night driving.

"When Ma and Pa went to Canada with the Oxford Group in the 30's, they travelled on the German ship Europa. Ma took to her bed before they left harbour; Pop, on the other hand, thoroughly enjoyed one of the worst storms the ship had met. Throughout, he and two others were the only passengers who never missed a meal. He told us that watching the huge waves breaking over the bow and hitting the bridge (where he had been invited to watch), was one of the most awe-inspiring things he had ever seen. (Sadly, I seem to have inherited Mama's predilection to sea-sickness).

"During the summers, before World War 2 we used to spend a month, either staying with Granny and Grandfather Denny at The Whins, near Bushmills, or in our own house at Portballintrae. Pop always loved the annual big all-day event when we would pile into cars and drive to White Park Bay. With his scouting background, Pop would take charge of setting up his 'cooking centre' in a suitable wind-free spot among the sand-dunes, just off the beach. We would collect rocks and Pop would build the fireplace while we hunted for driftwood. Then the big fun time, to half-fill a large cauldron with sea-water, going out far enough to avoid getting sand into it, to boil the new potatoes that had been dug that same morning. They were good Irish fluffy spuds; they tasted wonderful with lots of strong country butter – the best part of those memorable picnics."

The Oxford Group

So, in the early 1930's, we have the picture of the outstandingly successful Rector, running his huge Parish like clockwork, with his talent acknowledged by his appointment as Archdeacon. And yet, it is at this stage in his career, that Gordon recognises the need for a complete personal revolution in himself.

Some 5 years later, he wrote a draft manuscript of a book with the working title 'Any Parson', in which he speaks of the personal challenges which he had to face: – how they came about; how he learnt to deal with them; how he hoped that his experience would help others, who might be facing the same problems and difficulties which he had come through.

In the Preface to the book, he writes, " 'Any Parson' - that means me or you, or any of hundreds like us, anyone who has felt God's call to any position of leadership in His Church, such as we cannot shirk. I have put myself first, not that I have anything special to boast of, but because, if there is anything to be faced in the way of Christian Revolution, I must be prepared for it to start in me.

"In 1932, I was then, as I am now, in charge of one of the strongholds of our Church, in the midst of a keen and loyal people, and I know that the world was speaking well of me, but I was not satisfied. The sense of inadequacy of even our most successful activities in such a demanding world, led me to cross the water to attend a 'School of Life for Clergy' near Manchester. This was to be my first contact with the Oxford Group, and I wanted to investigate if these people had anything to teach me. I can never be too grateful for what I learnt there about myself, and for the new vision for Church and Country that naturally followed.

"The first real step in my education came when I saw myself completely in the dust, and someone there who loved me enough to take me and shake me free. My convictions were now crystallised into action. I had to take steps now for no other reason than that God directed them. I must obey or sell my soul. I saw that if Christianity was to be relevant it must be the genuine article, and that I must be prepared to have it applied scientifically to my own life and all its relationships. I was taught to recognise sin and how to deal with it."

When Gordon arrived at the Manchester gathering, he was slightly taken aback when he was asked by one of the laymen "What does it feel like to be constantly ten feet tall?" Gordon didn't follow. "What do you mean, ten feet tall?" "Well," came the reply, "you're six feet yourself and then there's the four feet of pedestal that you allow people to set you up on, and which you seem to enjoy!"

This kind of brightly-lit and somewhat brutal honesty was a new experience, but Gordon had come in the sense of enquiry, and he set about taking the next steps which he began to realise would be required of him. He decided that he would have to apply the practical principles of what he had learnt there to all aspects of his own life. He found that he had to face up to the challenge of the fact that his own wife, whom he loved very deeply, had no real or meaningful faith. He was convinced that this must in truth be a direct result of his own failure to communicate directly and honestly with her.

He decided that one of the first demands of his decision was that he should be truly honest with Hilda. What that involved was and is a matter entirely between them; it certainly is not a matter for us today. Whatever it meant, one direct result was that Hilda began to ask herself just what had happened to Gordon. He had been the unquestioned light and delight of her life; she herself had allowed him to live on the pedestal identified by the friend in Manchester; yet now here he was confessing his failings to her.

Never one to try to avoid a challenge herself, Hilda began to look at her own life. She was not overly happy with what she saw. She had played the role of 'the Rector's Wife' to the best of her ability, but without the depth of conviction that could only come from a personal faith. That thought and the answer to this quandary became unavoidable.

Gordon had told her that he had only realised his own need for change by getting down on his knees and offering the whole of his life, unconditionally, to God.

If that was something he needed and which had made such an astonishing change in him, she decided that it was something worth trying herself. With some apprehension, Hilda took the plunge and began to listen to what God had to say to her. God pulled no punches!

Hilda recounts the experience in her own words,

"Gordon was wonderful with me, and helped me to see that if I asked God, he would show me what to do. I wasn't too keen on this, but finally I said, 'O.K. I'll try anything once.' I certainly got a bucketful of thoughts about things I had to put right and I think that the Lord made Himself very real to me in sending me off to be honest with a woman in the Parish to whom I had told a whopping lie. I didn't want to see her at all and was scared stiff that my name would be mud all over the town; but it was quite clear to me that if I didn't obey God and take the first steps, I'd never get anywhere.

"So, cutting a long story short, the outcome of my visit to her was that she told me that she felt God must certainly have sent me to see her that day as she and her husband were desperately unhappy and were trying to see how best to get a divorce. I was green as grass in knowing how to help anyone in such straits, but I found she really wanted to talk and we finished up that afternoon together on our knees, with her giving her life to God. She apologised humbly to her husband for her bitterness and where she had been wrong. The next day her husband was down hot foot to see Gordon, saying he had never seen anything in the Christians of his acquaintance that moved him, but this seemed to be something different and he wanted to be in on it. Suffice it to say that those two people came to have one of the happiest homes I have ever known and were an enormous help to others."

Gordon's commitment to the Oxford Group and the challenge which it had presented to him did not prevent him from continuing with his existing duties in the ministry of the Church. The major difference was that he began to realise the importance of creating and training teams of people who were prepared to put their lives under God's control. This method of working was fundamental to the operations of the Group, and various 'Teams' who had been trained were moving in many parts of the world, taking their challenge with them.

In the early spring of 1934 Gordon and Hilda went, as part of an international team, to the United States and Canada. There they had the opportunity, for the first time, of making personal contact with Frank Buchman, the founder of the Oxford Group movement. While in Canada, the team received a great boost from the support of their work by the Prime Minister, McKenzie King.

Later, in the summer of that same year, a large team came to Belfast and a great public meeting was held in the Ulster Hall. The occasion drew big crowds; indeed, the hall was unable to accommodate them all. The Belfast Newsletter reported the event under the headlines: **THE OXFORD GROUP – A MESSAGE FOR IRELAND.**

Part of the long illustrated article read, "Under the auspices of an Oxford Group team which has been working in Belfast for some days, a public meeting was held in the Ulster Hall last night and attracted a remarkable audience.

"Ven. Gordon Hannon, M.A., Archdeacon of Dromore, who presided, said that in an hour of desperate world need the Oxford Group welcomed all present to study the whole problem of world-reconstruction. The salvation of Ireland would come as she saw and accepted and lost herself in her part in that great objective. The Oxford Group were a body of people, he said, who believed that God had a plan. Given the one condition of vital contact with God on the part of a sufficient number of individuals, His plan might become a reality."

Later, the report of Gordon's speech continues, "The Oxford Group is a Christian revolution for re-making the world. Recently, during a debate in the House of Lords on the world situation, Lord Salisbury referred to the Oxford Group, saying, 'What is needed is God-guided personalities leading God-guided nationalities to change the world.' In other words, re-make people and nations are re-made.

"Impolite people used to ask the impertinent question 'Can an Archdeacon be saved?' I stand here, thrilled with a new hope for Ireland and her destiny in a plan of world reconstruction, a hope which has come since I allowed God to demonstrate in me the fundamental fact that human nature can be changed. With that change, a hopelessness about Ireland and her problems has given way to an absolute conviction, demonstrated in almost every area of life, that Ireland can be re-built upon sound foundations as Irish men and women accept their part in God's plan for re-making the world."

Other speakers included General Hugh Montgomery, who later went on to found the Irish Association in 1938. The Association is still an important meeting ground for Irish people from many different cultures and personal interests from all parts of the island. The Rev. Dr. Macmillen, Moderator of the General Assembly of the Presbyterian Church in South Africa also spoke. He had met Frank Buchman's team when they visited his country, and he had been working to try to achieve reconciliation between the Dutch and British elements which had lasted as a festering sore on the community ever since the bitterness arising from the Boer Wars.

Over the course of the next five years, various teams grew up in different parts of Ireland including Dublin, in Belfast and of course in Lurgan itself. Gordon became well-known as a speaker and often attracted the crowds. Canon John Barry, a student at Trinity College Dublin in those years recalls "If you wanted to be sure of a full house for an S.C.M. meeting in TCD, all you needed to say was that the speaker would be the Archdeacon of Dromore. He was not only a fine-looking man; he had charisma!"

In the manuscript of 'Any Parson', Gordon makes one thing very clear: "The Oxford Group created no new loyalties for me, but helped me to understand that the worth of every loyalty is enhanced as men learn to make it completely subject to their one supreme loyalty to Jesus Christ. What I see clearly is that there must always be some place where Christians can be in complete fellowship, a united army; that where the Church is not 'a Mighty Army', it is not the Church of God."

'Any Parson' gives a wonderful insight into the philosophy which had driven him along his way in the years since he first became involved with the Oxford Group. Undoubtedly it was also designed to set out the challenge which he believed every clergyman should be prepared to face if he hoped to make the maximum impact with his ministry.

As a conscientious clergyman, Gordon had always fulfilled his regular daily Christian commitment to prayer and Bible reading. Now he found himself challenged to examine the whole pattern and practice of his life, using four standards of assessment: **Absolute Honesty; Absolute Purity; Absolute Unselfishness** and **Absolute Love**. These were not to replace his Christianity; they were not to become the be-all and end-all. Rather they were, and are, to be used as weapons in the hand of Jesus Christ, in helping every man in his constant struggle with human sin.

It is little use arguing as to whether there is such a thing as Absolute Honesty. With Jesus, Yea is Yea and Nay is Nay. His standards are absolute, and can be used as an inescapable yardstick against which to measure our own, certainly fallible, human performance. Gordon writes of each in turn.

"Absolute Honesty: I am faced with the first question. Have you been honest with yourself about yourself? Have you been honest with those you love best, about everything – even about the things when honesty crucifies pride? *Here the Cross appears, possibly for the first time in my experience. There is no compulsion about it except on the basis of discipleship. I am a free man either to accept the Cross with Him, or to refuse it and cease to play with discipleship."*

Gordon carries on, referring to many of the sorts of things that may come to mind - lies told to save ourselves or others; examination days; wearing masks to suit all the different people you like to please; financial questions - Tax Returns, expense accounts. Nothing is too small to be noted. The ultimate truth, and the whole secret about the application of an absolute standard, lies in one fundamental thesis:

'When man listens, God speaks.'

Dealing with *Absolute Purity*, Gordon writes of sex as nothing of which to be ashamed or afraid, but as something to be understood and adjusted under God's direction, as any of our other instincts. Experience has opened his eyes to the fact that only a small percentage of apparently happily-married people have their sex life properly adjusted, and so are strangers to what God has prepared for man and wife. God introduces us to an antiseptic purity which is the only answer to the amoral decay surrounding us.

Gordon expands the concept of purity to other areas of self-indulgence. He describes his own reliance for years on a cigarette or a pipe, to soothe unsettled nerves or any other disturbance. Most of us members of the family are too young to remember his 'smoking days', but Gordon often told of the day he settled himself to write a sermon and his pipe was missing. Chaos reigned. The whole household was put to the search. Suddenly, he stopped everything to ask himself the simple question, "Can't I do God's work without the help of a lift from a pipeful of tobacco?"

He didn't suddenly believe that everything he had done before – with a pipe in his mouth – was suddenly valueless; but he did believe and act immediately on the realisation that there would be no further need for that totally selfish indulgence in the days to come.

"God quickly showed me that here was one of His ways of giving me that training in disciplined living which I knew I needed." He never smoked again.

When man listens, God speaks.

Considering *Absolute Unselfishness*, Gordon recommends the possibilities of using a scientific approach, through which God can help us. Simply open a good dictionary and *let God take us through* all the words beginning with 'self-.'

Writing, as he is, for himself and his fellow-clergy, Gordon identifies both senses of inferiority and superiority as 'damned, evil-smelling selfishness such as nailed Christ to the Cross.' "Isn't it strange" he asks, "that people so often fail to recognise shyness, nervousness, ill-at-easeness as things of the 'self' that can cripple good work and hold up God's purpose? I remember so well what a difference it made for me when I realised that sensitiveness to criticism was sin, an obvious sign of life centering on self."

Later he writes "I remember the shame of the day when I thought I was fully surrendered to Christ, and, suddenly, I located in myself a tinge of satisfaction that the results I seemed to be getting compared more than favourably with those of a certain Rector in another Parish."

He writes of the dangers of 'possessiveness'. *My* parish, *My* Church, *My* people, *My* wife, *My* family. He remembers when his daughter Ruth came into the study, and he began telling her of the importance of keeping *'my study'* tidy. To which she promptly replied "But, Daddy, its not *your* study, it's *God's* study!" Another lesson learnt.

Under the same heading, he also writes, "Many a time I used to pray, and quite earnestly, 'O God take me, if need be break me, and make me all over again in Thy likeness.' I never realised what a terrible prayer that is until He took me at my word!"

When man listens, God Speaks.

Finally, in this section of his book, Gordon writes of *Absolute Love*.

"Men of good will are wrestling today with this problem: - Who can create enough red corpuscles of good-fellowship to counterbalance the white corpuscles of fear, hate, greed and suspicion? Can it be said with truth that the Church of Jesus Christ is Love in Action, as was obviously true of her Master?

"This standard faces me with straight issues. Is there any person for any reason whatever to whom I cannot give the love that is of God?

"So I take this self of mine through an unpleasant course of Spring-cleaning. The searchlight of God must search down into all the dark corners, the grudges, the jealousies, the resentments; those whom I have forgiven but cannot love; those who do not want my forgiveness and are not concerned whether I speak to them or not."

Later he asks, "What is my attitude to other Creeds or Denominations? Have I enough of the Christ Spirit to surrender everything in the way of defensiveness in my dealings with them? Am I as keen on helping a Presbyterian, a Methodist or a Roman Catholic, and sending them back to their own Church with new life, as I should be with one on my own register?" Gordon ends this section with what he describes as some lower school questions, including;

What is my temper like?
Do I love people enough to hold them to the highest?
Have I a passion for souls? Where is it in action now and with whom?
Do I spoil people – particularly in my own household?
When people are not in power, do I bother to think out with them their next step?
Am I willing to be challenged on any point by any body? By a layman?
What kind of pride is my chief temptation? - Face? Place? Race? Grace?
Does my particular point of view unite me to other Christians or raise barriers?
Have I criticised people? If so, who? What does God want me to do about it?
Have I ever stolen a character - or listened with interest while one was stolen?
Have I ever been sorry for myself?
Whom do I try to please in the pulpit?
Are my reactions similar when friends enjoy my sermon as when they criticise it?
Do any of these questions annoy me? —— **WHY?**

When man listens, God Speaks.

Before moving on to reflect, in this brief form, on the other sections of Gordon's book, it is interesting to realise how each of the four standards, in the order they are presented, fully subsumes the previous one. Purity clearly involves Honesty. Unselfishness, in its insistence on the wrongfulness and sin of self-indulgence, equally clearly leads to Purity. And finally, St. Paul reminds us inescapably of the totality of Love, which was clear and absolute in the words of Jesus himself. "Love God and Love your Neighbour."

In case of any doubt about the validity of *absoluteness*, remember the drum-beat of the words "with all my heart, with all my strength, with all my mind and with all my soul."

Right at the beginning of his book, in the Preface, Gordon says, "To some who speak at times of 'Group Methods', may I say that I have yet to meet the person whose life was transformed by Method or System, or anything else so simple."

Nevertheless, after outlining 'FACING FACTS' in Part One of the Book, he knows that there are certain disciplines which can make the implications and obligations of Facts Faced, clearer and more effective for Any Parson (or, indeed, any person) who is seriously setting out along the path of allowing Jesus Christ to take control of his life.

Three key elements of this disciplined approach, which Gordon goes on to examine and explain in Part Two of his book, can be summed up in the words 'Quiet Time', 'Guidance' and 'Sharing'. The title he chose for Part Two is 'UNDER AUTHORITY'. In it, Gordon explains how these three concepts can give as firm a foundation as possible to helping to make the decision to submit to Christ's authority.

On *'The Quiet Time'* he writes,

"The biggest change I had to face was a completely new discipline in my devotional life." *(remember that this book was written basically for Clergy)* "Not that I had been deliberately careless about it; I had tried hard, and experimented with all sorts of ways and means. I knew that there was little power in my devotional life that was not vitally connected with the boundless resources of God, through Prayer, Bible Reading and Sacrament. My trouble was that my plans always suffered from crowding-out, interruptions which it seemed impossible to avoid. When I faced facts, I was ashamed to think of the actual time per day, or week, spent alone with God.

"My decision now was an hour before breakfast. This was drastic for me as I had considered half-past eight a fairly reasonable breakfast-time for anyone with my busy life. For a time, it meant a real struggle, and it does still – the moment indiscipline is allowed to creep in; but the hour with God brings the rest and peace which the world cannot give.

"The reactions, in every department of life, were revolutionary, though natural. I began to discover a new worth in life. Experience has established for me the absolute necessity of a disciplined early Quiet Time, an appointment made with God which must not be broken, a time to be alone with Him, made possible because He is not particular, because He is willing to lodge with a man who is a sinner."

Describing the pattern of the hour, Gordon says, "My first duty is to realise that God is there to meet me." He then describes how he begins with a prayer, in which he surrenders control. Something along these lines:-

"Take O Lord and receive my liberty, my memory, my understanding and all my will; all that I am, all I possess are yours. You gave them to me. Now I give them back to You. Give me your love and grace, which are enough for me, and use everything of me according to your will."

Prayer is followed by Bible reading. As Gordon says, he is constantly reminded, from Bible reading, just what can happen when men listen to God and obey his commands. "I know that God speaks, and that if I went to the Bible, seeking his will and prepared to tune in and receive it, He would not disappoint me. I learnt to apply His great principles to the simple details of daily living. It soon became apparent to me that God had more to give me than 'nice thoughts'. He wanted His life carried out, in all my living and relationships. The fundamental approach to Him was, 'Speak Lord, for Thy servant heareth.' I have found it essential to have a book in which I keep a record of these daily times. It is a good spiritual barometer, and also I find it useful to refer to, many times during the day, possibly to renew the sense of God's presence, certainly to remind me of definite duties to be done. Writing down what God teaches and directs has been a great aid to real concentration, and the exercise of all His gifts of intellect and will-power."

The Quiet Time, as Gordon describes it, is the clearest example of 'When man listens, God speaks.' Gordon knows, at the same time, that man's frailty and sinfulness can interfere with the reception of God's word. Depression, irritability, criticism, dishonesty, lack of obedience to earlier decisions, - all can disrupt communication. As he says, "God teaches you that there is no virtue to be found in being over-tired or over-stressed, which are usually the fruits of unguided living.

"The Quiet Time is a time of vision for myself and all with whom God gives me contact, for my Church, for my particular part of the Church and for my Country. Too often, what men have called vision has been something which has left them in the clouds; they gave the place which belonged to vision to slushy sentimental dreaming. The vision which leaves a man in doubt about the next step towards his objective, and without the courage and determination to take it with confidence, is a mirage to lure well-meaning people further into the desert. So my time with God will leave me with quite definite steps on the unexplored journey of each new day."

Gordon then writes of **Guidance** and **Sharing**. When he was writing of the Quiet Time, he constantly underlined the value, not only of listening to God, but of making a record of the results. These written records of guidance received are a useful tool in making sure that instructions, received through 'listening', are neither forgotten, nor possibly selectively ignored, because they are too difficult or too demanding or too frightening. All these entirely human reactions to personally shattering instructions are constantly waiting for the chance to interfere with the communication channels.

Such instructions, or thoughts, or decisions received while listening to God, are generically described as *'Guidance'*, and it is important to realise that 'Guidance' is not something that can only be found during a dedicated Quiet Time hour, set aside before breakfast. Many times, over the years of living at home with Gordon and Hilda, when a crisis had arisen, or even a simple decision had to be taken, one or other of them has been heard to say "Let's have guidance about this". This was never some secretive, magic concept. For each of them, it was a simple and straightforward application of their dedication of their lives to God's service, by being ready, not only to seek His help and advice in a situation, but by being ready to react to, and act on, whatever God chose to say to them.

Returning then to his book, Gordon underlines the need for and the value of *'Sharing'*. He has already pointed out the ways in which our human personality and our human frailties can interfere with our communication channels to God. What he also knows, through personal experience and through observation, is that people, including himself, can become stubborn in refusing to **hear** - even when they listen, and even when they know that God has something to say.

Instead, they adopt 'selective hearing'. This technique is familiar to many people living in families where someone is recognised as being 'hard of hearing'. In spite of the handicap, it never ceases to amaze how, sometimes, they can apparently hear something quite clearly when it suits them, yet never hear something that doesn't fit in with their own plans. Exactly the same thing can easily happen when man sets out to listen to God, even in a genuinely dedicated Quiet Time.

Human frailty can introduce selective hearing. God speaks, Man listens and then chooses to record only the things he wants to hear. Now, what is written down has all the weight of 'Guidance'. "I have written it down, therefore it must be all right!" This can lead to dangerous self-deception.

As Gordon suggests, everyone knows examples of people, be they Clergy or lay, who have set out with enormous enthusiasm to tackle a project which they are convinced is the right thing to do. Their enthusiasm is genuine, but, too often, the motivation can be suspect. Are they hiding a call to do something else behind a curtain of 'busy-ness'? Are they seeking the approval of other people? Are they, in the first place, the right people for the job in question?

Everyone can recognise the scenario, but how can it be coped with, if the person involved insists that it is a matter of following God's Guidance? This is where the value of the concept of *'Sharing'* comes in. While he recognises the existence of the negative element of the practice and thinking just expressed, Gordon is led, logically, to underline the positive elements of the Fellowship which Sharing can create. A planned sharing of thoughts received under Guidance, and a checking of their validity, can create bonds between those involved, and provide enormous support to those who make the initial commitment to put their lives and their future fully into the hands and under the control of Jesus Christ's positive inspiration and direction.

If a newcomer to the concept of committed self-examination is horrified or frightened by what is revealed by the crystal clear searchlight of Christ's challenge and teaching, there is great strength to be drawn from the support of the human being who has brought that newcomer to the threshold of this new life.

This support is of special value when the one who has already undergone the experience of deep personal change is ready to share the depths to which he or she, personally, was required to dig. It also underlines the strength experienced and available, by drawing on Christ's unlimited love in dealing with whatever challenges have to be faced, and are waiting to be overcome.

On the subject of **Quiet Times**, **Guidance** and **Fellowship**, Gordon writes,

"Possibly some may still have occasional doubts about the value of this time with God, and of life lived on such a basis. The main reason for such patches in my own life is plain laziness. Probably at the root of that is unwillingness to get guidance, or to pay the cost of being tuned in to receive it, or, what both of these amount to, unwillingness to obey it. Our little girl put it quite plainly one day, when the question of Brussels Sprouts was under discussion. 'No, I don't want to have a Quiet Time, for I know what God would tell me.' Nor is it the guidance which we can't get that worries, but rather the guidance we can't avoid. This recalls Mark Twain's saying about the Bible, that it wasn't the parts of the Bible he didn't understand that worried him, but the parts which he did!"

Gordon summarises this part of his book under the one heading of 'Authority'. He says, amongst other things, "What is happening in other lands may at any time happen to the Established Church as we know it.

"It is not difficult to see that the axe is already being laid to the root of the tree. All the signs of burning churches are in Ireland. Although religion has a firmer grip than in many other places, people qualified to judge see her as one of the danger spots of the world. There are enough conflicting loyalties to disintegrate any land unless they find one supreme loyalty that will purify them and give them value that is eternal.

"It is a strange phenomenon, in a land so proud of its Christianity, how very difficult it seems to be to realise that Jesus Christ alone can enable man to be his best self, and that complete surrender to Him is the only door to abundant life – true for the individual, and equally true for institutions and for society. So long as men's view is bounded by an almost fanatical loyalty to an institution, in theory or in point of view, anything of vision for the country as a whole is out of the question. These things have a way of working out their own destruction.

"The solution of Ireland's problems is certain as, one by one, men allow Him, first of all, to make them according to His purpose. Then, in an amazing way, all the jumbled pieces of orange and green and other colours begin to find their place and value in His masterpiece. The challenge from a friend from another land is, 'Demonstrate the Kingdom of God in Ireland and the problems of World Peace will be easy'."

In Part III of his book, Gordon looks at the two concepts of Training and Ministry. He begins by outlining five steps to the 'Life-changing' experience. He sums them up as the five *'C's'* – Confidence, Conviction, Confession, Conversion and Continuance.

On **Confidence**, Gordon writes, "Someone put it this way to me, and it sums up a great deal. 'It is just as great a sin to try to change a man, without making friends with him, as it is to make friends with a man, without trying to change him!' Always in the background, is the fact that we have an experience of God that means so much to us that we cannot contemplate the tragedy of anyone trying to face life without it. We only need to be honest."

He continues by describing how convincing someone that *'human nature can be changed'* will lead that friend to the **Conviction** of that possibility which, in turn, will pass naturally, through facing the challenges of the four Absolute Standards, to a **Confession** of the results. "These two stages are sometimes summed up as Sharing."

Gordon goes on: "Having been along the way ourselves, we can be used as guides. The whole human story has to be related to the supreme fact, the fact of God as revealed in the Cross. God's forgiveness, God's love, God's life – God willing, and God able, to take the whole wretched mess and make of it a new creation. Here is the critical stage called **Conversion** – the transaction between the human soul and God, of which we are allowed to be a witness."

Later he writes: "There then remains the further stage, often by far the most important, of **Continuance**. Helping the 'babe in Christ' to relate to his new experience, as he is called to live it, all comes under that heading. There is a need for living beside the new convert, helping him through his restitution, if all his new life is not to drain away before he ever understands the joy of being an effective unit in God's redeeming plan. He must see something of the vision of what God could do with the absolute control of him. It is so essential to help him get the New Management recognised and established in all his contacts."

Gordon returns to the challenge for 'Any Parson'. He reflects on how Jesus spent much of His time on the 'Training of the Twelve', while still having time to care for, and speak to, 'the Crowd'.

"In the constant strain of a Parish, it is particularly difficult to balance the amount of God's time He wants spent on the Twelve, and on the Crowd. One lesson we cannot ignore; the Son of Man always had time for the individual."

Again, later: "In any little I've been able to do, in the training of either parsons or lay people, to pass on Christ's message to others, the most difficult thing has been to hammer out of them the desire to preach at people. When I faced the full challenge of Christ in detail, my first pledge to my people was that I should stop passing on to them good advice, of which I was convinced their pockets were already full, but that, with God's help, my message would be substantiated with the good news of what, daily, God was doing for me. God keep us from giving good advice to hungry people!

"I have often thought that there was something wrong with a system that compels a man to preach twice every Sunday to his congregation. To compel a man to go into the pulpit, who may not then be experiencing the victorious power of the Living Christ, seems the very negation of Christianity.

"If there is someone within the Parish with whom the preacher is not in fellowship, while he proclaims the Gospel of Love and Forgiveness, he makes that Gospel stink in the nostrils of the decent average pagan."

Again, as he writes of the development of Ministry, Gordon continues: "The day cannot be far distant when the laity will have the place God planned for them, as part of His living Body, with a real Priesthood. Then, in the fellowship which the Holy Spirit creates out of all those who believe in the Lord Jesus Christ, in sincerity and truth, leadership will go naturally to the spiritually fit – parson or layman.

"We have been trained in the atmosphere where those lay people, who were obviously designed to be spiritual leaders, have been gradually sidelined as Parish pack-horses. We have allowed our splendid lay people to think that their job was to make Parochial ends meet. Even this job has, as often as not, been passed on to the Parson, especially if he has more financial ability than spiritual understanding.

"Ordained men strain every nerve, too often over-straining them, in trying to overtake a task that was never meant for them – probably building up a martyr's reputation and preparing for an early grave, over which little more can be recorded!

"It seems so strange that the only Christian to visit the sick, in soul or body, should be the Parson. Why should he, only, have a message from God for his fellows? Why should he, only, have the responsibility of training forces for the Kingdom? Why should people with expert knowledge, and possibly unique spiritual experience, be condemned to listen, Sunday after Sunday, to the gallant efforts of possibly worn-out Rectors, or very junior Curates? It passes all human understanding among a people who are praying constantly for 'a right judgment in all things'. A wealth of human material has been completely lost because we Parsons have dug ourselves in, in our authoritative position.

"As a test of what I mean: supposing there is a change of Rector, in how many parishes will the new man find a Fellowship of trained people, who can give him an adequate picture of where the front line of the Kingdom is running, in their own lives, and in the community as a whole, and a picture of the immediate objective, and what forces are available for capturing it for God?

"To be a Parson today, demands that a man shall not only have a living experience of Christ himself, which gives him an adequate answer to all human problems, but surely it also demands the power and the willingness to have the discipline which will enable him to train leadership.

"Parochially, as a Diocese and as a Church, it is time we stood still and asked ourselves honestly 'What is it all about?'

"My conviction is that, from the moment a man feels anything in the way of a Call to the Ministry, someone should be available to show him how to get himself and his living under God's control.

"I can remember days when, though I was really keen on my job as a Parson, I was shy of the company of those whose experience of Christ was red-hot. I remember feeling ill-at-ease and defensive. Such experiences give me real sympathy with the man who has accepted the position of spiritual leadership but who has never been given the fellowship in which he could face the full challenge of Christ. I find it difficult to understand the Parson who has the opportunity of facing that challenge and turns it down, but still remains a Parson.

"I can imagine nothing more like Hell than that!"

Before leaving Gordon's book, it is worth looking at the later chapters, which contain much of what could be described as his vision of where the Church of Ireland might move, and of how it should grow.

"I picture the early group of Christians in Jerusalem planning, every man with his special responsibility. This age of specialisation need not spoil the picture, provided we ourselves, and our individual specialities (our first concern), are under the control of God. I see Paul and Barnabas, separated for teamwork. Here is real vocation – 'It seemed good to the Holy Spirit and to us.' I see the Church of Ireland planning salvation and new life for Ireland. The right to save Ireland is her heritage. Our first concern is sufficient numbers of Christians, fully released and available for God, determined, at any cost, to bring the country, every part of it, under God's control."

[This last paragraph clearly indicates that Gordon is becoming increasingly aware of a call to a wider ministry in his own future]

"I have seen that, by planning and working together intelligently, in the discipline of teamwork, under the guidance of the Holy Spirit, miracles can happen.

"When I was a Curate in Dublin, I was greatly impressed by some of the things that I saw leading up to the Rebellion of Easter 1916. I am not concerned here with the wrongs or rights of that whole ghastly business, but what does bring conviction is what men, with fanatical enthusiasm that made them count not their lives dear to them, actually accomplished, in bringing about a complete revolution. The Challenge to us is what can our life and witness as a Church show, in this day and age.

"The Church will provide inspiration for statesmen, rather than criticise them, inspiration and programmes so compelling and constructive, that either statesmen will be 'changed', or they will be compelled to make way for others who have had life-changing experience themselves.

"Man will begin to understand the sacredness of every calling in the fulfilling of God's plan, and the meaning of the Master's words – 'Seek ye first the Kingdom and His righteousness, and all these things will be yours as well'.

"A Church which brings Parliaments under God's guidance will be His natural instrument for saving and inspiring the Government of the nation. It makes me toe the line to realise that the Church is the soul of the community, the soul of the Dail and of Stormont, the soul of industry, medicine, education, civic life and sport, the soul of the home, the kitchen and the living-room. The responsibility of every Christian is the winning of his sector of the nation's life for Christ, and to think out intelligently, how it is to be brought under God's control. For that, he must be prepared to give his very life.

"The Church will naturally have a positive plan for every great force that moulds the thinking and living of the Nation, - the Press, the Stage, the Wireless.

"Such a conception of the Church revolutionises our approach to Ministry. My conviction is that the future will see far fewer men set apart for this work, because other members of the body will have taken back many of the functions which we parsons have usurped. Our job will be, as commissioned officers, to think through the forces at God's disposal, and help them see their part, and to hold them fearlessly to it. The Clergy will have to learn the art of decentralisation, surrendering more of their priestly function to a much wider constituency."

Gordon believes that many of the perceived *'problems'* of the Church are rather *symptoms*. If they are treated rather as simple difficulties in personal relationships, God's light would soon banish worlds of darkness.

Even as long ago as 1937, Gordon writes, "The problem of 'evangelism", which is getting such limelight, is resolved when Any Parson becomes the Evangelist of his own people and rallies his forces against the strongholds of the enemy, in the life of the Church and the Nation.

"Is there any problem of Church Building, or Parochial Hall Building, or indeed any other financial problem, which is not already solved, when everything that a Christian has is at the disposal of God? Will any of our problems be anywhere nearer final solution until that fundamental condition has been obtained? It is rather humiliating, in the 20th Century of the Christian era, to realise that we are still in the infantile stages of Christianity! We have accepted the theory, but refused the life."

"I pray for the courage of the Prophets, to hear God's voice and accept His call, and, in His name, to proclaim to a world in desperate need, **'Thus saith the Lord!'**

"The fundamental step in Christian leadership is the whole-hearted individual acceptance of this Gift of God, which makes all things new.

"Thus it is that a growing family of Christians in many countries is determined to allow a wave of absolute love and unselfishness to sweep through their land. *They will serve no other Master.*"

A Fresh Challenge

Throughout the 1930's, Frank Buchman spent much of his time travelling and meeting world leaders and opinion formers, particularly in Europe as well as at home in the United States of America.

On May 29th 1938, against the background of recent hunger marches, economic depression and a worsening international situation with widespread calls for military re-armament, Buchman spoke at a reception in his honour in East Ham Town Hall, London, cradle of the British Labour Movement. Calling for a programme of *moral* re-armament, in the course of his speech, he said:

"The world's condition cannot but cause disquiet and anxiety. Hostility piles up between nation and nation, labour and capital, class and class. The cost of bitterness and fear mounts daily. Friction and frustration are undermining our homes. The crisis is fundamentally a moral one. The nations must re-arm morally. Moral recovery is essentially the forerunner of economic recovery.

"We need a power strong enough to change human nature and build bridges between man and man, faction and faction. This starts when everyone admits his own faults instead of spot-lighting the other fellow's. God alone can change human nature. When men change, nations change. Leaders changed, a nation's thinking changed, a world at peace with itself.

"The average man wants to see the other fellow honest, the other nation at peace with his own. We all want to *get*, but with such changed leaders we might all want to *give*. We might find in this new spirit an answer to the problems which are paralysing economic recovery.

"Suppose everybody cared enough, everybody shared enough, wouldn't everybody have enough? There is enough in the world for everyone's need, but not enough for everyone's greed.

"God has a nation-wide programme that provides inspiration and liberty for all and anticipates all political programmes.

Gordon Hannon

"Only a new spirit in men can bring a new spirit in industry. New men, new homes, new industry, new nations, a new world.

"We have not yet tapped the great creative sources in the Mind of God. God has a plan, and the combined moral and spiritual forces of the nation can find that plan. We can, we must, and we will generate a moral and spiritual force that is powerful enough to re-make the world.'

From the time of this speech onwards, the Oxford Group began working under the name of Moral Re-Armament, frequently shortened to MRA. Frank Buchman launched large scale campaigns in an effort to awaken the democracies to the challenges posed by the dictatorships of Fascism, Nazism and Communism. 25,000 gathered to hear him speak in the British Industries Fair building in Birmingham, and there was a similar response when he went on to Holland, Norway, Sweden and Denmark. Gordon and Hilda joined him in Stockholm in August 1938, where Gordon preached to a packed Cathedral in the presence of the King and government leaders.

Buchman summed up his message to a Scandinavian Assembly for MRA held in the old Hanseatic city of Visby on the Swedish island of Gottland.

"We meet here as Christians, and our final authority is God's plan.

"We have come here with different objectives. First some have come here hoping to be changed ... very good, very necessary. Some have come with the hope that you will learn to change others. That, too, is very necessary. But the danger is that some of you want to stop there. I am tremendously interested in a third point – how to save a crumbling civilisation; how to reach the millions of the world.

"All these things ought naturally to follow each other ... but sin comes along. I don't know if you believe it or not, but it is here.

"Some of you would like a nice comfortable awakening, a revival. A nice, armchair religion. But to stop there is inferior thinking. The next step is revolution. It is uncomfortable. A lot of Christians don't like the word. It scares them. It makes them goose-fleshy. That's where some of your critics come from – goose-fleshy Christians with armchair Christianity. The point is this: are the Christians going to build a Christian philosophy that will move Europe? Are you that kind of Christian? Is that the New Testament?

"An increasing number of Christians in democratic states are now unwilling to acknowledge, in speech and action, those inner authorities on which the life of democracy depends. Each has his own plan … so wonderful … such freedom … such liberty. But, in a true democracy you don't do as you please, you do as God guides. You do God's plan.

"Some people in the Acts of the Apostles and the Gospels gave everything. Others did not. Even in a revolution, some want an amount of padding around them. If you want to be that kind of revolutionary, there may be a comfortable place for you behind the lines. But somewhere on the battlefront will be the real revolutionaries.

"You will do well today to read the 51st Psalm. And then the New Testament about the Cross of Christ. You will never, never, never come into this experience until you know the Cross of Christ. Not I, but Christ.

"The biggest thing this afternoon may be for you to go off alone and decide where you are going to stand. It is between you and God. A Deed, like a transfer of property, so that you turn over your life to God for full and complete direction."

When he returned to Lurgan, Gordon took these words to heart and a totally new challenge beckoned.

Note

All the statements by Frank Buchman, quoted above, and those quoted later on pages 106-107 are reprinted, by permission, from *Remaking the World* – the *Speeches of Frank N.D. Buchman* (Blandford Press, London 1961) © The Oxford Group.

For a fuller version of the 'East Ham Town Hall' speech and also the full text of an important manifesto called 'The Destiny of Nations' issued by Frank Buchman in 1937. See Appendix A

1939/1940 - Leaving Lurgan

In these early days of the 21st Century, it can be surprising to find that events which we remember as 'recent', are already being studied at school under the heading of 'History'. We do not often realise how fortunate we are to have lived throughout a period of almost 60 years, free of war on a global scale.

Look back 20 years from 2004, and what do we see? Margaret Thatcher as Prime Minister, the Falklands, Ronald Reagan in the White House, Michael Gorbachev in the Kremlin. Somehow it doesn't feel all that long ago.

Now if we place ourselves in 1939, we may perhaps begin to realise just how horribly real must have been people's memories of the 1914-18 war: the 'war to end all wars', the Great War or, as we call it today, World War I. In 1938, the British Prime Minister had flown to meet Adolph Hitler to try to preserve peace. 'Peace in our time' was the cry.

In spite of every attempt to stop it, the march towards the inevitable moved remorselessly on. Hitler's armies trampled on treaties as he dared his country's old opponents to stand up against him. He had convinced himself and his people that, this time, Germany would win. Eventually, the worm turned and an ultimatum was issued. The deadline for a reply was 11 o'clock on the morning of Sunday, 3rd September 1939.

I was 9 years old at the time, and the family were staying with Granny Denny. We gathered round the radio, waiting for an announcement from No.10 Downing Street. Eventually, Mr. Chamberlain's voice came through, and we heard the awful words "I have to tell you therefore that this country is at war with Germany". Gordon (my father), Hilda and her mother (our Granny Denny) stood there surrounded by the family – some too young to understand, all in our Sunday best, ready to walk to Billy Parish Church for Morning Service.

It was awful. I had never seen real-life grown-ups cry before. Even looking back, it is hard to imagine or comprehend the horrors of the thoughts that must have been going through their minds. In Gordon's family, in 1914, there had been 15 'Hannon' first cousins, 6 boys and 9 girls. By 1918, only 2 of the boys survived, Gordon himself and his older brother Rex.

On 3rd September 1939, no one was waving flags in the streets.

After the end of the Great War, medals were awarded to those who had served. Two sets of campaign medals, together with scrolls acknowledging the sacrifices made by Gordon's brothers, Leslie and Ion, were sent to his parents. The scrolls were framed together with the medals and, after his mother's death, they were hung in a place of honour, one on each side of the desk, in Gordon's study. They remained there for the rest of his life.

From his early days as a Divinity student, it was obvious that Gordon had an unusual breadth of vision of what an effective Christian should be, and of what he should set out to achieve. His experience and training with the Oxford Group helped him to widen that breadth of vision and to increase its depth.

After Frank Buchman launched the concept of Moral Re-Armament in 1938, it was no longer enough for anyone to settle for what might be called simple personal change. Gordon recognised the new challenge. He began to feel constrained by the limitations of his parochial and diocesan responsibilities. Of course they were important, and he never stopped challenging the individuals he met, to live their lives to the full, to hand over total control to God's guidance, in loyalty to Jesus Christ. 'To be the best that I can be'.

By the beginning of 1939, he was discussing the future paths to which he felt God was calling him with those closest to him and with the Bishop of his Diocese. On the basis of the responsibility of the thought 'As I am, so is my Nation', Gordon was convinced that the time had come to take his personal convictions and his message to a wider field. Bishop McNeice understood these feelings and was prepared to support them.

Gordon also talked everything over with Archbishop Gregg, then Primate and Archbishop of Armagh. Discussing his ideas for his future, Gordon said to the Primate, "Your Grace, we both know the size and the importance of my work in Lurgan Parish and the Diocese. Do you think that if, in the next few years, I could bring *three men* in positions of influence in the country to the place where all their actions were governed by God, it would be worth giving up the Parish?" The Primate thought for a while and then said, "If you can bring *one man* to that stage, it would be worth it for the country's sake."

In December 1939, just three months after the outbreak of the Second World War, Gordon finalised his decision. Under the headlines **'A Shock for Shankill' – Venerable A.G. Hannon resigns Rectorship – A Change of Activities,** the Lurgan Mail of Saturday 2nd December reported.

'The announcement made by the Venerable A.G. Hannon, M.A, Archdeacon of Dromore, in the Shankill Parish Magazine, issued on Saturday, and his pronouncement from the pulpit on Sunday morning that he had decided to resign his office as Rector of the Parish and Archdeacon of Dromore, in order to concentrate upon the Moral Re-Armament campaign in Ireland came as a surprise to his parishioners.

'Archdeacon Hannon was appointed Rector of Shankill Parish in 1924. The Parish is one of the largest in the Church of Ireland, and its Rectors have, and are recognised as exercising, a wide sphere of influence in the Church government, and have been selected not only for their administrative ability but also for their qualities of mind and heart and as good shepherds of the flock, and Archdeacon Hannon was no exception to the rule. The care of approximately 6000 souls calls for an amazing amount of unremitting pastoral labour.

'In recent years Archdeacon Hannon was attracted by and became one of the most ardent advocates of the Oxford Group Movement, and to this he devoted a measure of his time, including the campaign for Moral Re-Armament. These are projects of great importance in the Christian world and any man who feels that they open a door to wider spheres of service must, if he has the courage of his convictions, face up to them.

'Not one of his parishioners for a moment doubted that Archdeacon Hannon was not a man of courage, and he has now proved it by resigning a good living and bright prospects in the Church in order to study and further the cause he has so much at heart.

'Archdeacon Hannon, in the administration of the Parish, gained the respect, goodwill and esteem of his parishioners, especially for his sympathy and help in their hours of sorrow, difficulty and trial.

'To sever connections with friends; to leave a home which abounds with very many happy recollections; to resign a source for steady income in a world of uncertainty; to wage a campaign for God and the world calls for courage of the highest order and strong faith that God will provide for the morrow.

'No matter what individual members of the congregation may think of the purposes their Rector has so much at heart, they must individually and collectively admire his bold and courageous step which deep-seated conviction has now induced him to take, and they will follow with deep-hearted interest his work on behalf of the campaign for Moral Re-Armament.'

After outlining the details of his career in the Church's Ministry, the newspaper goes on to give a full report of Gordon's farewell sermon given on the previous Sunday. Though reported in the Lurgan Mail in the third person as 'he said', that sermon must have sounded as follows.

"Today I do not feel like preaching a sermon, but I recognise that what I am going to do is made easier by knowing that I stand in the midst of many good friends.

"On Friday evening last, I informed the Select Vestry that, in obedience to a very persistent Call to a wider sphere of service, I had found it necessary to give to the Bishop my resignation from the rectorship of Shankill Parish and of the Archdeaconry of Dromore, and that the Bishop had accepted it.

"This was no sudden decision; for the past twelve months, almost, I have been checking the genuineness of the Call with the highest authorities of the Church, and I do not think that there has been any doubt in the mind of anybody that what I see before me is a genuine Call from God.

"At the moment there is no place for such a Call in the official constitution of the Church of Ireland but, none the less, I will have a full licence from the Bishop and I hope to be free to officiate anywhere I am needed.

"Our new house will be in Belfast and I do not need to tell you people here what my message is. Many of you are seeing the insistent need for learning new lines of approach to the tremendous problems that are being intensified by war.

"I look back to the experience of the last war, and I cannot help remembering that two of my brothers, 200 men from Shankill Parish and millions of others gave their lives in that war – and yet to a very large extent that sacrifice was in vain – Why? Because those who were left were not spiritually fit for peace.

"Now I look ahead, as all responsible people must look ahead, to the problems that will follow this present war – problems that we can see already. As we look at every country in the world, we see how Institutional Religion has been going through crucifixion – in Russia, in Germany, in Spain, in every country, and woe be to those who refuse to see the signs of the times and to learn the lessons that God is giving us the opportunity to learn.

"Last Friday evening, the Earl of Athlone broadcast from London to the whole Empire on Moral Re-Armament. He put it this way 'The choice today is between Moral Re-Armament and national decay'. Next weekend, December 1st, 2nd and 3rd the objective will be 'One Hundred Million Listening to God'. A world force that will make future war unnecessary.

"A call to citizens is being made by responsible authorities all over Great Britain and Northern Ireland; not this time by Church authorities, but by more than 200 Lord Mayors and Mayors, as well as chairmen of Local Authorities, to their fellow citizens to take up the Call.

"I am glad to say that, in our own land, more and more people in responsible positions are understanding that they must take responsibility for their own vocations, whether business, education, local authority or any of the great callings; that they must take responsibility there, to get these great forces under the control of God; to see what contribution they could give to their country; to see that their country could make her fullest contribution to the family of nations.

"My wife and I have been feeling very strongly that God has been training us to help the men and women occupying those responsible positions to see the highest way they could give their lives to God for his control. The vision we see before us is an army of men and women, glad and willing to give their lives, their homes, their jobs and all their relationships to be, as completely as they could make them, under the control of God.

"We can understand what a tremendous responsibility such a Calling means. Last Sunday evening I spoke to you from this pulpit on 'Why Jesus chose the Cross'. I did not know then that it would be this Sunday morning that I would have to tell you of my resignation. But we saw last week that Jesus chose the Cross because he was out for a great objective, and because, in seeking that objective, there was no alternative.

"I like to think that you, the people of Shankill Parish – my best friends – will think of what I have told you this morning as good news which I am passing on; not because I have to sever my connection with this great Parish which has meant so much to me, but because a man sees clearly what is the Call of God, and that you and we have the privilege of making this contribution to the life of the country.

"The people of the Parish are sending out their sons and loved ones gladly, to lay down their lives, if need be, for King and Country and for the cause of peace. They know, or at least they are beginning to understand, that the real war is a war waged in the realm of the spirit, and that the battlefront is here in Lurgan – in their own houses, in their own personal living, and that they have the responsibility of deciding whether the Front Line is being held for God or for the forces of disruption.

"We all have to learn a completely new sense of responsibility. My own conviction is that, for too long, we have been playing with Christianity. There has been too much talking about it, and not enough living it.

"My decision has not been a personal decision only: it is a family decision. Some people at Friday's Vestry meeting wondered about the future of Shankill Parish. My answer was very simple – that the same thing applies to the whole problem of a man's home and his children. Some people said that a man has the right to make a decision for himself or his wife, but what about the children?

"I believe that many of you here today have got beyond that stage; you understand that when God calls a man, He will look after all the facts and circumstances surrounding the Call. Those of our children old enough to understand are absolutely with my wife and me in this thing – even though to them, on a human basis, it looks like risking their future. My own conviction is that this is the biggest thing that could happen in our children's true education. After all, are our children any more important than the children of other parents – the children of Poland or Germany, the children of Spain or of China?

"The basis of true democracy, which we so constantly talk about, is the simple fact that every man is of equal importance in the sight of God, and their true destiny is realised under His control.

"So we are looking forward to being backed up by many friends from Shankill Parish, by their prayers and by their co-operation, for we will be one with you in many ways. Many Parishes are willing to give their Rectors to go out to serve with the Forces. The parishioners of Shankill Parish would willingly give your Rector, for the time being, to go out to that particular service. I am convinced that if you stay close to God, He will show clearly what His great purpose is for the Parish. I pray that God will send you a successor who will carry on the traditions of your beloved Parish.

"I cannot for a moment pretend that my decision has not been a very costly one, and most of all I feel the parting from so many true friends. I am not saying 'Goodbye' today. I have had a wonderful 15 years in Lurgan and I thank God that many wonderful things have happened. I have made many mistakes. Nobody has been more conscious of them than I. But God has been good."

In January 1940, Gordon and Hilda stepped out together into a future based on the total conviction that they were doing what God was calling them to do. Without any support, other than their faith that God would provide, they set up house in Belfast.

Wolfhill

The House

In 1940, in the early years of the Second World War, Northern Ireland had three major economic strands supporting its existence. As in the rest of the island there was an extensive farming industry, mainly dependent, in the North, on flax-growing, potatoes and cattle and sheep farming. There was also some rather limited cereal growing. In the Belfast area there was a very considerable element of heavy industry, with such giants as the Harland & Wolff shipyard – at the time, the largest single yard in the world, the Belfast Rope Works – again, the largest in the world, and several major engineering works such as Mackie's and the Sirocco Works. Short Brothers & Harland's were building aircraft in their plant beside Belfast Harbour. And then there was linen.

In all parts of the Province you could find communities, often whole villages and even towns where the only employment available, apart from what are now called 'service industries', was to be found in one of the great linen works. There were the spinning mills and the weaving factories; there were all the specialist firms throughout the area turning out the finished manufactured products, all of which proudly bore the label known throughout the world – Ulster Linen.

Scattered across the countryside stood villages where the Mill was the whole reason for their existence. The mill-owners lived in the Big House; the workers lived in houses built specially for them. When the Mill Hooter blasted out in the early morning, practically every door opened, as one or more of the family set off to work. It was no idyll. The work was hard and the hours were long, but there was a tremendous sense of community and belonging; everyone knew everyone else.

Like many other big cities, Belfast had grown steadily in the 19th and into the 20th century, and in the process had absorbed many of the little villages which had formerly had their separate existences outside the city boundaries. One of these was Ligoniel on the slopes of Wolfhill to the north of the city. Wolfhill Spinning Mill was one of the traditional establishments and, in the grounds beside the mill, a long avenue led from the comparative poverty of the Ligoniel Road to the Big House. There were four houses altogether on the way along the avenue. First, a modest house by the main gate, then a slightly larger house occupied by one of the managers at the mill; third came a fine villa with its own gardens where the Managing Director, Mr Malone, lived. Finally, at the head of the avenue, stood Wolfhill House itself. Set in superb, beautifully maintained and extensive grounds, the house belonged to the owners of the Company.

When Gordon made his decision to resign his positions in the Church and to commit himself on a full-time basis to the work of Moral Re-Armament, he did so in the full knowledge of the fact that he would no longer have either the good salary or the free house that went with the job as Rector and Archdeacon. Where would he find somewhere suitable for carrying out the task he had set himself?

The old hymn tells us that 'God moves in a mysterious way' and this now proved to be the case for Gordon and Hilda. Shortly after announcing his decision, Gordon was invited to preach in Belfast Cathedral. There he outlined his plans for the future and the basis on which they depended for success. He was putting his trust in God to support his purpose and was prepared to go forward on the basis of 'faith and prayer'. As Hilda recalls, "Many people were deeply moved, and a few days later a businessman offered us the use of a huge house called Wolfhill, at a nominal rent, complete with free electricity and a supply of coal from the Mill at only fifteen shillings a ton."

This was truly a remarkable answer to prayer. The house was immediately available because the Mill-owning family was living in India. Gordon and Hilda were able to move in by the end of January 1940, less than two months after Gordon had announced his decision to leave Lurgan.

As Hilda said, the establishment was indeed huge. The house itself had four large reception rooms, ten bedrooms, a complete self-contained two-bedroom flat, numerous pantries and larders, a workshop, a wash-house and, finally, what was to prove enormously useful later, a great ballroom, some

Wolfhill House

1940 an early group L-R Peter, Will Davey ,David, Leslie Ruth, Alec Russell, Vi Strong, Brian, Hilda, Gordon, Philip Thompson, Arnold Wedgewood, and Lance Montgomery.

1600 square feet in area. The extensive gardens were well looked after and the greenhouses produced beautiful peaches and a steady supply of tomatoes through the summer months. There were two mill dams in the grounds, both well stocked with trout and both available to the people living in the house. When he had the chance to relax, Gordon was able to get out his favourite rod and spend time on the quiet banks of the dams recalling those early days of his youth on the River Barrow.

Beginning in Belfast

With the facilities offered by the house, it immediately became possible for Gordon to begin building up the solid core of an 'MRA team' in Belfast.

Over the years since the Oxford Group first came to Ireland, many fresh people, both in the North and in the South, had decided to put their lives fully under God's control. In most cases, this did not mean an abandonment of existing jobs or responsibilities; rather, with many, it meant offering control, not only of personal life, but of every aspect, including the workplace, the factory floor, the office, the classroom, the business, and the interpersonal relationships in all those situations, to the direction of the guidance of God.

All these people were conscious of the need to keep their daily lives and their decisions under guidance and they recognised the need for support from others of like mind if they were to do so. As a result, there were frequent meetings for the sharing and checking of guidance and for the preparation of plans for the effective spreading of the message. These 'team meetings', as they were called, were a regular feature of everyday life. But, because they were working to no particular co-ordinated plan, it sometimes happened that groups tended to concentrate on special interests for special situations without realising the greater possibilities that would arise from a more inclusive overall concept of the best way of making use of the available manpower.

It was a major part of Gordon's thinking that the creation of a strong central unit, still totally under God's direction, would greatly increase the effectiveness of the MRA presence in moving the country forward. That was the principal new dimension that he was bringing into action.

With his experience of leadership within the ministry of the Church, Gordon was recognised as having a natural talent as a leader both in action and in thought. When his decision was taken, he had the full support of MRA people in all parts of Northern Ireland and in the South. This was underlined by the remarkable decision of Sydney Gibson, a Dublin businessman, to make a generous regular contribution to Gordon's financial situation over the following years. Sydney was one of the senior partners in the printing firm of Bailey, Son and Gibson and, himself, had met the Oxford Group three years earlier. He was one of those people who decided that the best way forward for him, was to continue running his business, while at the same time allowing God's control to take the major place. This meant running the business on the basis of absolute honesty within the firm and also in dealing with his customers.

In a letter written some time later, when he had been helping Gordon financially for some seven years, Sydney wrote, "The investment of this money was the best bit of business I ever did! Look at the dividends! I have no money outside my home and my business; all else I invest in M.R.A., and I do wish that I could learn how to get businessmen everywhere to see that here is the only sure security. Riches are, I think, the greatest source of worry and certainly prevent many from entering into the kingdom of heaven, where men are free. I am grateful for what I have learnt about stewardship since first I met the Oxford Group."

Meanwhile, at Wolfhill, the family, together with Florrie Dowds, settled in. Soon, several people who were committed to MRA felt it right to join Gordon and Hilda in their work. Amongst the earliest were Bill Page and his sister Dorothy, both of whom were deeply involved with the work of the Presbyterian Church, Dick Laughlin, Kathleen Montgomery, and Rose Walker, who came to offer her services as Gordon's secretary. All of these made their home in Wolfhill. Other regular members of the core team who carried on with their daily working lives but contributed to the thinking and planning in those early days included Dr. Lance Montgomery, Ellie Uprichard from Lurgan, and Alec Russell, a Belfast solicitor. There were many others who contributed time, talent and effort over the following years.

Some former colleagues in the Church of Ireland found it hard to understand why Gordon had taken the decision to leave his parochial and other work. Some resented the fact that he seemed to them to be saying, in effect, that he had found something more important to do with his life, thereby downgrading their own calling. This was far from Gordon's mind. Others, at all levels, realised the importance of his work. Among them were Charles Tyndall, Bishop of Derry, Canon Arthur Gordon (later Dean of Rosscarbery), and the Rev. Billy Allander, who, in 1943, followed in Gordon's footsteps by becoming Head of the Trinity College Mission. These men all worked constructively with him, while he also had continued backing and support from the Archbishop of Armagh.

During the four long years of the 1914-18 Great War, Gordon had made several attempts to get directly involved as a Chaplain. As mentioned earlier, these efforts came to nothing as each in turn was frustrated, either by Church authorities or by changes in Gordon's responsibilities. Now in 1940, Gordon felt that at last he was in a position to make a direct contribution to the war effort. Any guilt which he might have felt about 'letting the side down' in those earlier years could now be eliminated by the conviction that he was doing his bit.

Although born in Co. Kildare and brought up in what was later to become the Republic, Gordon had spent almost all his working life in Northern Ireland. As a member of the Protestant community in Ireland, he had inherited a sense of loyalty to the established British Empire as he grew up. (He must have rejoiced at its later development into a British Commonwealth of Nations, staying together voluntarily, even as the imperial control was released.) This loyalty remained with him all his life although it never prevented him from identifying himself proudly as an Irishman. Now his whole personal moral strength was put into helping the national war effort.

All over Britain, contact had been made with local government authorities in an effort to raise national morale. In Belfast this plan was also launched with the support of the Lord Mayor. A Morale Card was distributed to 100,000 households in the City. The challenge was clear.

THE CALL TO THE HOME FRONT

MRA

WHAT I CAN DO

I **PLEDGE** to God and Country my fullest service in this hour of need.

PLEDGE to my Neighbour consideration equal with myself, his family with my family.

PLEDGE to my own Neighbourhood that I shall take responsibility in practical ways . . . .

MY HOME will be an asset not a liability.

MY HOME will thoroughly understand what to do in Air Raids, will know the nearest First-Aid and Fire-Fighting Centres, and will follow all official instructions.

MY HOME will co-operate with neighbours so that when an emergency arises we shall do what is expected of us.

MY HOME will build up the morale of children, by enlisting their help and encouraging them to observe an evening Curfew.

MY HOME will be a Rumour Decontamination H. Q., where old rumours are rendered harmless and new rumours are critically examined.

MY HOME will consider the problems of the community, obey the rationing orders in spirit as well as in letter, and pay promptly for goods.

MY HOME will try to make the problems of Government easier.

THE Strength of a Nation is Moral Re-Armament, the only force which can make the National effort adequate and keep our motives clean.

The Secret of Steadiness and Inner Strength is to Listen to God and to Do what He says, Therefore

I PLEDGE MYSELF TO A CODE OF LIVING centred in GOD.

CONFIDENCE	that cuts out	FEAR.
THOUGHTFULNESS	....	GREED.
CHEERFULNESS	....	GROUSING.
DISCIPLINE	....	SOFTNESS.
UNDERSTANDING	....	PREJUDICE.
SALVAGE	....	WASTE.
PREPAREDNESS	....	REMORSE.

The centre of the Empire's Flag is a CROSS.

I PLEDGE MYSELF to work to put that Cross in the centre of the Nation's life.

The Nation that "doeth the will of God abideth for ever."

Message from the Rt. Hon. the Lord Mayor of Belfast
(Sir Crawford McCullagh, Bart., D.L.) :—
"I heartily commend the above Call to every citizen of Belfast and sincerely hope each one will live up to the letter and the spirit of the Pledges set out therein." 13th July, 1940.

Copies may be had from M.R.A., Kingscourt, 17 Wellington Place, Belfast

Challenges and People

It was the generosity of one of the great linen companies that allowed Gordon and his family and the MRA team to have their base at Wolfhill. It was an interesting coincidence that 1940, the year Gordon moved to Belfast, was to prove to be the year which became a time of fundamental change in the whole linen industry.

After years of gradually building up a solid base of trade union membership among the women workers in the mills, their leaders decided that the time had come for a trial of strength with the employers. Led by Saidie Patterson, the redoubtable Secretary of the Textile Section of the Amalgamated Transport and General Workers Union, and with the backing of the largely male members of the other sections, a demand for recognition of a closed shop was made to the management of Ewart's – at that time the largest weaving mill in Belfast.

For years, the women workers in the mills had been dreadfully exploited. Long hours, poor wages and the harsh working conditions made life a constant drudgery: a weaver, one of whose looms broke down and was idle through no fault of her own, would find her wages reduced. Paid holidays or even paid sick leave had never been considered. Times had to change. David Bleakley in his book about Saidie Patterson tells the story in detail. He includes an interesting fact: Ewart's, although chosen as the battle ground, were by no means the worst of the employers.

From their point of view, many of the big linen companies honestly believed that they were doing a fundamentally good service by providing work for the poor and under-privileged in their communities. They built, owned and maintained the houses in which their people lived. As long as there was a market for their products, there would be work to be done. The hard times of the depression years had not been their fault. Of course they wanted the people to have work; the people were their people; who needed trade unions? - they were only trouble-makers. As good long-standing employers who had built up their empires, they didn't need instructions from the factory floor.

The scene was set for a mighty battle.

For seven long weeks the strike ran on; Ewart's was effectively brought to a standstill. Bitter words were exchanged, with, on one side, the Company suggesting that the workers were betraying the interests of friends and relatives serving the country in the armed forces. Saidie Patterson replied in a message to the strikers, "The employers have challenged our loyalty. We know your loyalty too well. Our fellow trade unionists have joined the fighting forces to give battle to those who have destroyed trade unionism in Germany. We know them better than your Directors... Don't permit anyone to destroy their unions while they are away at the front."

Both sides received criticism from the press, since things were going badly in the War for the allies. Eventually the strike was ended without the total victory on a closed shop demanded by the union, but with many concessions about wages and conditions from the Company. What had changed in Ewart's soon became standard practice in the rest of the industry and comparative peace returned.

There were other difficulties in other parts of the industrial scene in Northern Ireland and this whole area became one on which Gordon began to focus major effort. He made firm friends with Bob Getgood, who was the leader of the ATGWU in the North, which meant being involved in many of the areas where problems were likely to arise. Physically, Bob was a tiny man, but his size was more than matched by an enormous personality and a native capacity for leadership. Years of experience at the head of union activity had brought him to the edge of accepting the full ideology of the international communist movement as the answer to industrial problems.

Gordon knew that if he could convince Bob of the greater answer available from handing control of his life to God's guidance, Bob would become one of those he had set out to look for. Under guidance, negotiations would move from a constant battlefield of 'Who's right?' to the constructive attitude of 'What's right?' – on both sides of the table.

The first challenge in their discussions was to convince Bob that making such a decision would not result in him becoming a less effective leader of the trade union movement to which he had dedicated so much of his life. The next challenge, on the other hand, was to Bob himself – to have the courage to commit himself to the ideas Gordon was presenting and to take the plunge. Being the man he was, Bob never did things by half-measures. Either he was in or he was out. He took the decision to throw himself into a life led by God and waited to see what would happen. His courage was never in doubt and it was to be sorely tested by the attitude of many of his associates who believed that the decision would result in him going soft. They didn't know their man!

Another man whose potential was recognised by Gordon at the time was Graham Larmor, head of The Ulster Weaving Company. There is a fascinating correspondence, mainly from him to Gordon, but also containing drafts of some of Gordon's replies. Graham Larmor is very consistent in his attitude to Gordon's approach to industrial affairs. He writes, "You have my sympathy in your effort to find a new way for many people to express themselves in matters of religion and method of living, such as is much needed, and which the Churches as the ordinary 'thinking' person knows them, do not provide entirely, but so many things have to be done by persons like myself in the 'daily grind' – particularly in carrying-through of the War-effort – which one knows to be 'not quite cricket', but nevertheless essential, that I would feel a frightful hypocrite if I attempted to pose as having high ideals while knowing full well that I was not in a position to carry them out from hour to hour."

Later, in the same long letter, he writes, "There is a great deal wrong with the Churches as a whole, and their methods, but there is also a great deal wrong with the World in general, and if your efforts can strike home to the latter more forcibly than the Churches as we know them are doing, you certainly deserve all the encouragement possible to give."

In spite of this basically non-committal reply, Gordon maintained contact with Graham Larmor for more than twenty years, gradually forging a close personal friendship with him. Larmor however always made the point that, while he admired the philosophy, he was not prepared to pay the personal price which would be involved in a total commitment to it.

Gordon with Bob Getgood at Wolfhill front door

R-L : Gordon, Lily Thompson, Harry McKee and his wife, Fred Thompson MP

Two other men became close friends in the early years at Wolfhill. Harry McKee, the Editor of the Belfast Newsletter, was a self-declared atheist who became a regular visitor. Gordon felt that Harry's position of responsibility in the main newspaper serving the Unionist community in Northern Ireland meant that his attitudes were of vital importance in building up a positive drive among the people towards the war effort. Once again a personal situation arose where Harry was prepared to listen and, often, to take advice about the needs of the nation. Even though he never made any formal personal commitment, Harry gradually found again, for himself, the re-awakening faith of his original upbringing, and he was delighted to be asked to become a godfather to Michael, when Hilda produced the last of her six children in 1942.

Michael's arrival coincided with another significant moment in the family's history. Leslie had left school in 1941 and, had completed his first year engineering course at Queen's University. He planned to volunteer for service in the Royal Air Force after that first year. Gordon was away from home at the time, on one of his frequent visits to London, where he was in constant touch with those who were co-ordinating MRA activities across Britain. On the day that Leslie actually signed up with the RAF, Hilda realised that the new baby was on the way. In Gordon's absence, Leslie drove her to the hospital. Michael arrived early the next morning, and Leslie just had time to see his new brother before catching the evening boat to Liverpool, that same evening.

Michael writes "I have often asked myself why I was born at all – six years after Brian and in the depths of wartime. Mama used to reassure me that I was carefully planned. Les intended to join up in the autumn of 1942. With Pop having lost two younger brothers in the First War, did he and Mama fear the worst and decide to have me in case Les didn't come back? Anyway, there I was, born on September 23rd 1942, the very day Les set off to join up. Pop had gone to London a few days before – a risky trip in itself – and heard the news of my arrival on the phone. He was sharing a room with Harold Grotrian, a man of no small means, who agreed to be a godfather and promptly wrote Pop a cheque for £1,000, a substantial sum in those days, to help with my future education."

1698386 LAC Hannon NL (Leslie) with Michael

Hilda, Brian, Gordon and his tomatoes

Hilda at the piano with some of the gang

Michael 'shaving' Gordon

In addition to Harry McKee, the other person with whom Gordon was to spend a great deal of time, both during and after the war years, was Fred Thompson, Unionist MP at Stormont for the Ballynafeigh constituency, who also owned and ran a large laundry firm in the City. Fred and his family all became fully involved with MRA, while continuing with their other responsibilities. This contact with Fred and with Bob Getgood meant that Gordon was able to help with negotiations between management and unions in that industry, and to set an example of the effect of new attitudes in maintaining good relationships between the two parties, without weakening the values or responsibilities of the positions taken by either side.

In later years, when Bob Getgood was elected as a Northern Ireland Labour Party M.P. at Stormont, this continuing relationship between the two men allowed them to discuss political decisions, about which they held differing views, on the basis of 'What's right?' rather than 'Who's right?' – an unusual concept in Irish politics on any side of the Border!

It would be quite wrong to suggest that these concentrations on individuals in Belfast were the only things happening at Wolfhill. Gordon continued to gather an ever increasing team.

When Frank Buchman first came to Great Britain, he visited Oxford University where he enlisted a number of students who believed that the challenge he was offering was the most important idea they had ever met. They joined him on a visit to South Africa, and, on the journey, someone identified their baggage by a tag reading 'the Oxford group'. This was the source of the movement's original name.

Gordon may well have had Frank Buchman's example in mind when he went down to Trinity College in Dublin. He met a group of young men who were already in touch with the philosophy and ideas of MRA through the work of David Telford. David was an ex-World War 1 pilot and accountant who had changed a lifestyle of a bottle of whisky a day, Portmarnock Golf Club, and generally being 'one of the boys', to committing himself totally to a life under God's control and God's guidance. He and his wife Panny were both working on a full-time basis, particularly trying to help the younger generation who faced all the temptations of student life.

The generosity of men like Sydney Gibson and Harold Grotrian was a good example of the answer to the question, "Where does the money come from?" which was often thrown at MRA by its critics, as a smear, suggesting that there were some mysterious influences behind its activities. Gordon's own views on the subject of the financial basis on which he was working are well summed up in a page from his personal notebook.

Principles that govern Finance.

"When I belong to God, that involves everything that I am and have, my poverty or my wealth, my contacts. Nothing in me must complicate the matter of His control of me and my neighbour. I think of myself and the Other Fellow constantly at our highest in God's service. I think of my country under God's control and my value is my power of creating that control – also my neighbour's. If he has wealth he has correspondingly higher responsibility. It is not his any more than mine is mine.

"The world will rapidly destroy itself under any other plan than God-control. Therefore it is the only secure investment.

"My real security is trust in God and His children who acknowledge Him. Money is second only to sex as power. In itself it is neither good nor bad, it is merely raw material and it depends for value or liability on who or what controls it."

David Telford had led the team of students to accept the discipline and challenge of applying their personal faith in an active way to their daily lives. Eric Turpin recalls the battles they had with some of their more rumbustious student neighbours who mocked their genuine and overt Christianity. On one occasion they were meeting in Roddy Evans's rooms where they had been joined by Cyrus Walsh, the Captain of the University Rugby team. The rooms directly overhead belonged to a member of the Boat Club who set out to try and disrupt the meeting below. The noise level steadily increased until Cyrus decided to sort things out. He went upstairs and knocked on the door. History doesn't record exactly what he said, but the effect was complete: a suitable degree of quiet descended.

Eric remembers the first meeting with Gordon. "Suddenly our team found themselves offered the challenge of a wider vision. What the world needed was men and women who realised that their personal convictions could take on a much wider significance. Deep personal conviction and dedication was the essential basis on which to build. Without it, any house that was built would indeed be built on sand. Gordon was asking us to take the next step. This was a direct reflection of Frank Buchman's vision that MRA needed to transform a personal faith into a world concept."

Inspired by Gordon's challenge, several of the student group came up to Belfast and became regular members of the team which Gordon was building at Wolfhill. In addition to Eric Turpin himself and Dr. Roddy Evans, others who came from Trinity included Muriel Barrett and Bill Porter. Dr. Ken Stewart was another TCD man who had many contacts with Wolfhill – particularly when he was working as a House Surgeon in the Samaritan Hospital in Belfast. He remembers "enjoying Hilda's generous hospitality and Gordon's readiness to listen to our experiences. He always gave us wise counsel without being critical or judgemental. We would return with fresh vision and commitment. Gordon was an inspiration to us all, especially when the going got tough."

Although it means taking a backward step in time, it would be a pity, when writing of Trinity men who played an important part in Gordon's life, not to have mentioned Tom Shillington. Tom first met the Oxford Group in 1933 or 1934 and was a good friend of Ken Stewart. Tom was very keen to be a journalist and was already writing when he was a student: Harry McKee thought well of his work. He was an enthusiastic oarsman and enjoyed the student life to the full. When he decided to take up the challenge of God's absolute standards and apply them to his own life, he found himself constantly receiving the word 'work' at the top of the list in the guidance coming to him during his Quiet Times. Eventually, he realised that this message was clear, and he set himself to studying for Moderatorship in Classics. This meant a complete change in lifestyle, with ten hours solid study in the day.

After Trinity, Tom went to England for a period of concentrated training at the Oxford Group Headquarters. He regularly came back to his home in Northern Ireland where he and his sister Edith worked together, helping to give inspirational leadership to the Team which was building up in Ulster. They became close friends with Gordon and Hilda. When the War broke out, Edith was in America.

Tom joined up in the Royal Armoured Corps at their base at Tidworth. He wrote, "One of the great secrets I have learnt is always to ask God's purpose as I move into a new situation." In his first five months at Tidworth he and a friend introduced some four hundred men to the idea of vital Christianity, and when he moved on, he left an organised team to carry on.

He was posted to the Middle East, where eventually he was killed during the Battle of Alamein. In one of his last letters he wrote, "I was very grateful my letters had been used so much in Trinity. I shall often think and pray for the Team there. I found it very difficult to live under guidance there. Life was a struggle. This morning I read *Mark Chapter IX* on top of our tank as the sun rose: 'Everyone will be salted with fire.' That's one for me, and the next one is for all of us, especially TCD: 'Have salt in yourselves; have peace one with another.' Ireland may escape the fire of this suffering, so make sure you have plenty of salt!" On the evening before his death, in his guidance, he wrote, "Determination. It all starts with determination to overcome the simplest difficulties of daily life. As ever, the greatest thing in my heart is that a new spirit will come quickly – the spirit of Moral Re-Armament, bringing 'the will to conquer' - the foundation of a new world."

Much of this story of a remarkable young man comes from a memorial address preached by Gordon in Trinity College Chapel on December 12th 1942.

Over the years, Gordon had made contact with many leading personalities in the South. He met Maud Gonne McBride, the legendary Republican whose husband had been executed by the British for his part in the 1916 uprising. In the course of an early conversation, he discovered that she was writing a book about the current Irish situation. She told him that she was in the middle of a chapter dealing with the Orange Order, giving it a thorough slating. Gordon told her that he himself had been a member of the Order. At once she ran out of the room and summoned her family so that they could actually see a real live Orangeman!

Roddy Evans tells the story of another of Gordon's significant contacts in his book 'Where I Sensed The Breath of God'.

"From this base *(Wolfhill)*, he reached out to the political and civic leaders in both parts of Ireland, and a great variety of people rallied to his leadership and initiative.

One of these was Lord Hugh Beresford, a prominent member of the Anglo-Irish community, for whom Gordon Hannon arranged a visit to Eamonn de Valera in Dublin, and Gordon accompanied his friend at that meeting. More than 40 years later, The Irish Times in March 1984, carried the following report:

Father Michael MacGriel S.J. revealed that President de Valera told him of an Anglo-Irish peer who asked to meet him around the beginning of the Second World War. His visitor told the President that he regretted very much the hostility between the Anglo-Irish Ascendancy and those who set up the new Irish State and their passivity in relation to public life. He promised that after the war, he would offer his services to building up the Irish State. The impact of this noble gesture so impressed de Valera that he felt he, for his part, would welcome such support. Unfortunately, the peer was killed in action but his offer had a lasting effect on de Valera.

Lord Hugh Beresford died while serving with Lord Mountbatten on H.M.S Kelly when the destroyer was sunk by enemy action in 1942."

Developments At Home

Most of 1940 was spent in settling in and building the team into an effective unit. By the beginning of 1941, Gordon spent much of his time working with industry on both sides of the negotiating table. One of the firms where he had constant contact was the Faulat shirt factory, run by James Faulkner, father of Brian Faulkner who later became the last Prime Minister of Northern Ireland. The Faulat factory was heavily involved in making uniform shirts for the armed forces and, like many other establishments in Northern Ireland, had been accustomed for years to management who believed that their methods were in the best interest of all concerned, whether in the Boardroom or on the factory floor. With the demands and pressures of being involved in a part of the war effort, many in the trade union movement knew that their position had been suddenly strengthened. Industrial relations across many industries became strained. The linen industry was not unique in this area.

Gordon was determined to do everything possible to support the successful outcome of the War, and he realised that industrial strife was doing nothing to help in that purpose. At the same time he realised that he must not be seen to be 'taking sides' in any factory conflict. He was determined to convince management and unions that the most efficient way of dealing with disputes was for both sides to enter negotiations with their ambitions clear, but also with a willingness to realise that neither had a unilateral right to get everything their own way. James Faulkner was a tough nut to crack: he believed that he knew how to manage his company. Similarly, those representing the workforce were convinced that things had to change. With Gordon being seen to talk to both sides, and to be supplying the same standards of advice to both, it became possible for honest and fair agreements to be reached.

In April 1941, the comparative peace and disassociation of Belfast from the War came to a sudden and horrendous stop with the first of the two great air raids to hit the City. Wolfhill House itself was built into the side of the mountains, north of the city, and, unless one of the German pilots had been specifically sent to try to bomb it, was one of the safest places to be. However, things were very different in the city itself.

Looking down from the house, Gordon and Hilda could see the flames from the burning buildings lighting up the sky. The next day the full extent of the damage could be seen. No one had believed that the Luftwaffe would be able to reach Belfast and there were few defences of any sort to react when the bombers arrived. The obvious particular targets for the raids were the shipyards, the aircraft factory and the industries in East Belfast, although, as in many other cities in the UK, there were many bombs dropped indiscriminately in other areas.

One couple who had known Gordon and Hilda for several years in Lurgan days were Denis and Nora Hanna. Before they were married, Nora was a teacher in Lurgan College and she became a close friend of Hilda's. Denis was a young architect who was working for his father's firm with branches in Dublin and in Belfast.

At the time of the Blitz, they were living at Wolfhill. Denis had a job with Belfast City Corporation's Architectural Department, but both he and Nora were also among those working solidly with the MRA team. During the air raid, Nora, who was expecting her second child, suddenly announced that the baby was on its way. Gordon offered to drive her to the hospital through all the chaos, but the baby actually arrived in the back of the car. Not surprisingly, Gordon was treated by the hospital staff as if he was the father! One of the nurses said to Nora, "Your husband looks the image of Archdeacon Hannon." Nora replied, "That's because he is Gordon Hannon." To which the nurse replied, "Never mind, dear, we'll soon get you sorted out!"

After the first raid, one of the cellars at Wolfhill was strengthened to convert it into a shelter where the family could take refuge. When the second raid arrived in early May, Gordon and Hilda both felt that they ought to do something to help. They set off down into the city and found a scene of total pandemonium around the big primary school in the Ardoyne area which was supposed to be a rest centre.

No one in authority had turned up to open the building, so they forced the door to let the injured folk inside. Hilda began by helping to clean up the badly burnt face of a baby that had been blown into a fireplace, while Gordon used his Scouting training to give help where he could. When one of the women began having a baby, the people around all thought Gordon was a doctor and Hilda a nurse.

Hilda's memoirs go on, "We didn't disillusion them and tried to deal with everything as it came. After what seemed a terrifyingly long time more help came and we got the dead collected in one place, the worst injured in another, while the others, not so badly hurt, helped with the rest, although many were so badly shocked by all the bombs that they could be of little assistance. I remember we commandeered a car and took the mother and baby to hospital where we were greeted by a young doctor who took one look at me and burst into fits of laughter at the sight of me – black with soot and messy with blood and other things – I'm afraid I thought his mirth ill-timed!"

There were no more serious raids on Belfast, but the brutality of those two nights still has an impact on memories today. Gordon suffered badly from the after-effects of his experiences. A combination of physical and nervous exhaustion resulted in an unpleasant attack of shingles which covered most of his body. Hilda had to stand him in the bath and scrub him all over as part of the recommended treatment at the time. It was an agonising process.

After the two air raids, the people of Belfast felt much more clearly involved in the war. Although there was no conscription in Northern Ireland, many men and women had joined the forces, but they had 'gone away to the war'.

In the Spring of 1941, the war had come to Belfast – with a vengeance!

The team in Wolfhill now began to work on two parallel programmes – one of what today would be called ideological training seminars and the other the preparation of a dramatic revue called 'Battle Together For Britain'. In spite of the fact that Russia was under attack from Germany and was now one of the Allies, it was clear to Gordon and others in MRA that there was an organised plan under way for Communist Party members to take over the leadership of the trade unions and the labour side of industry. The totalitarianism of their ideology was as unacceptable as the Fascism of Germany; each was based on its own materialistic godless philosophy. In the course of the seminars, a major part of the ideological training combined the basic essential of living under God's guidance with the analysis of the concept of ideology itself.

Any ideology needs three fundamental elements – the three 'P's' – a Passion, a Philosophy and a Plan.

Anyone looking at either of the two great materialistic ideologies can easily see each of the three elements. Fascism's philosophy of racial purity, its passion for national superiority and its plan of taking over the world.

In the same way, Communism's philosophy of class war, its passion for destruction of capitalism in all its forms and its plan, once again, for world domination. Many people found irresistible attractions in both of those ideas. Why did they have to be faced up to and challenged, and how could such a challenge be soundly based? These were the scenarios studied in the seminars and the questions asked.

Gordon left one archival loose-leaf notebook containing a wide variety of pieces of guidance, notes for sermons, outlines for lectures and analyses of challenges which reveal much of the heart of the message delivered at those meetings held in Wolfhill. Some pages are headed **MRA. What is it?** They include:-

The yardstick by which men and nations are assessed.
(a way of life that answers the problems you read about in newspapers)
An Ideology – to create a world force to remake men & nations
An Organism
A Revolution
Based on Absolute Moral Standards – Not enough!
1. Needs **A Passion** Born of
    Decision of will to put God in charge
    Conviction – Realisation of where I need to change
    Total honesty with at least one person
Lenin said 'Remove the myth of God from the mind of man'
William Penn said 'Man must decide to be governed by God or inevitably he will condemn himself to be ruled by tyrants.'
2. A Philosophy
Study RMW *(Author's note: This translated to Remaking The World – the book of speeches quoted earlier in A Fresh Challenge. After searching again in that source, the following passage was found)*
"A new world philosophy is needed, a world philosophy capable of creating a new era of constructive relationships between men and

nations. A new statesmanship and a new leadership will ensue from this heightened quality of thinking and living. This world philosophy will emerge as people begin to get their direction from the living God. It will be within the framework of a hate-free, fear-free, greed-free quality of living."

Gordon's notes continue:

A dynamic in 80 countries

Know your facts through and through. Tell your leaders.

Materialism uses men to develop an idea; MRA uses an idea to develop men.

3. *A Plan* MRA What Is It?

It is the way of personal freedom and fulfilment

It is against nobody, nor set of people

It provides an incentive from within

It unites people

It is scientific: it goes to the roots of problems

It is experimental – anyone can try it now

It begins with me, my home, my industry, my party, my nation

It breaks the vicious circle, dealing with human nature thoroughly and drastically on a national scale

It is the alternative to war, to man's historic road to violence and destruction

It is the way of national defence, because it is the way to win the respect of neighbours

It is the answer for industry uniting all sections for a world of abundance for all

It is the answer youth is looking for – the only adequate one – the opportunity to give everything for something great

It is the answer for family life – the way of freedom and responsibility that cuts out dictatorship

It is the secret of education because it has the secret of how to live together

It creates an irresistible force, free to remake the world

It forges amiable individuals into a united force on a constructive plan

It is the constructive answer to subversive forces because it changes
them and deals with the selfishness that creates them
It is a new dimension of thinking, caring, living
It is what we are, rather than anything we do
It is people before things

This list of separate points is well worth reading several times over, if
only because it underlines the universality of the application of the basic
principles of MRA. The people who came to the meetings at Wolfhill came
from all sorts of backgrounds – from business, from both sides of industry,
from politics, from ordinary homes, from schools and colleges, from
anywhere where problems could arise. The amazing thing to see happening
was that they all were presented with the same fundamental answer, and
that, in so many cases, they found that the same answer applied to their
individual situations.

Gordon used to say that there was little to be gained by telling someone
who needed change that they were wrong. The only way to convince them
of their need was to be able to show them an idea bigger than the one already
running their lives.

Asking the question 'What's right?' in a situation, combined with the
concept that 'When man listens, God speaks', could lead to remarkable
consequences. People so often found themselves facing a challenge which
came from within – whether from God or from elsewhere was for them to
decide. Even when working with agnostic or atheist, Gordon would ask
them to try the same technique of quietly listening, with an open mind, and
being prepared to write down the thoughts that followed. He used to say that
many men and women came to the decision that they could not manage on
their own, and, even with the non-believers, were prepared to get down on
their knees and 'give God a chance'! It was a philosophy of life in action,
summed up in ideas such as – 'As I am, so is my nation.'; 'If you want to
see the world different, the best place to start is with yourself.'; 'God has a
plan and you have a part.'; 'God has the answer to every human problem –
if you are prepared to ask Him what it is.'

These seminars all took place in the great ballroom in Wolfhill which had been converted from an enormous playroom for the family into a small intimate theatre. In earlier days, and even more so later, when we were to move house to Greenisland, where there was a big old hay barn, many energetic games of a form of indoor hockey (known as 'hurkey') were played – particularly between Peter and myself. Due to my somewhat unpredictable temper, these were not always carried out in the best spirit of traditional British sportsmanship!

On one infamous occasion, Gordon and Hilda were entertaining a man who had important responsibilities and connections in the newspaper world and in Unionist circles. He had come to visit with his wife and two sons. Peter and I were told to look after the boys and we took them upstairs to the Ballroom. There a furious row erupted between the two of us, while the visitors looked on. Hilda was not at all pleased when she came up to call us all down for tea, and found us giving a perfect example of what could happen when the concept of Absolute Love was clearly not being practised by the junior members of the family! We were both in disgrace.

Part of the daily pattern of life at Wolfhill was family prayers after breakfast. This pattern continued, even when the household increased in numbers. First a Bible reading, then, after prayers, a communal Quiet Time followed. Everyone, including the children, had a notebook to record any guidance. For the grown-ups, this was a vitally important element of their professed life, and it gave a pattern to the rest of the day.

Ruth, one of the younger family members at the time, remembers, "We often had Quiet Times to look for God's guidance for daily living and for the world around us. I was never expected to conform but I always found that trying to find God's direction was by far the most adventurous and interesting way to live. Dad gave me a simple steer: '(1) Is there anything to be sorry about? (2) Is there anything to be thankful for? And (3) Think of the things you might do in the day ahead and the people you work or play with.'

"That simple faith, through family life, through keeping honest and giving your best, in whatever field, stayed with me throughout the ups and downs of life. It was a commitment through my teenage years and gave me a solid foundation for life and has led to a wonderful variety of experience and friends, for which I shall ever be grateful. It was always a challenge to think wider than myself."

Brian also remembers the family Quiet Time, sitting round the kitchen table after breakfast, always a time of listening to God, listening and sharing together, often saying the General Thanksgiving as well as the Lord's Prayer and the Grace. "I never had any difficulty with the concept of God as a merciful loving Father, because I had just such a loving father in life."

Others sometimes found the communal Quiet Time stressful because there was a need to contribute something as the sharing of guidance moved inexorably round the table. This pressure was perhaps one of the less effective parts of the way MRA sometimes operated with young children. They did not seem to have worked out the best way of handling the relationship between the generations. There was never any question of a lack of love: but there was, on occasion, a tendency to use the Quiet Time as a substitute for other forms of discipline.

Even Brian, in spite of what he has already said, tells of an occasion when he had been caught in the act of trying to steal money from Hilda's coat pocket. Instead of giving him a smart smack on the bottom, Hilda suggested that the two of them should have a Quiet Time about the situation. Brian remembers sitting there, already guilt-stricken, accepting the justice of the obvious outcome, and simply wishing she would get on with it!

In my own case, I remember one particular day when I had been very rude to Hilda. A family outing to the cinema was planned for the same evening and the suggestion was made that a sensible punishment would be to leave me behind. I complained bitterly that it wouldn't be fair, so Gordon suggested that the family have a Quiet Time together to decide what should be done. After a time of quiet, he asked me what my guidance was. Undaunted, and eternally optimistic, I said, "My guidance is that I should go to the pictures with the rest of the family." Unfortunately, no one else's guidance agreed, and I did not get to see the picture. Ah, well!

It is interesting that Peter and his wife Fiona, both of whom have been dedicated full-time MRA workers, decided that they would never try to use the idea of a 'Quiet Time' with their girls when family discipline was involved. Gordon and Hilda had found MRA such a refreshing and rejuvenating power in their own lives, that it never seems to have crossed their minds just how forceful its application could be to someone who had not had enough life experience to comprehend the full potential of its influence.

While the seminars in the ballroom continued, work was also going ahead to construct a stage at one end of the room. The place was big enough to accommodate an audience of about 60 people. A stage door access was built on the outside wall so that the cast could use the huge old laundry room below as a dressing and make-up area. An exciting revue called 'Battle Together For Britain' had been written and performed in various parts of Great Britain. Now the plan was to run it in Belfast. Some material had to be adjusted to suit Northern Irish accents and dialect, but rehearsals soon got under way.

It was a remarkably ambitious project since few of those who took part had any dramatic experience. However, it is not a matter of looking back through rose tinted spectacles, when the revue is remembered as a stunning success. The show featured a wide variety of scenes.

A family situation dealing with rationing and food shortages and rows between husband and wife

A heritage scene with portraits of famous national and international people coming to life under a spotlight and delivering stirring speeches such as Elizabeth I at Dartford "I have the body of a weak and feeble woman, but I have the heart and stomach of a king, and of a king of England too."

A parade of cooks, brandishing wooden spoons, singing "We're the arm behind the army..."

An industrial scene featuring 'Miss Trust', played by Vi Strong from Southern Africa, wearing a stunning scarlet suit and spreading divisive rumours amongst workers and management

An evil Chief Rat, supported by a gang of little rats, gloating over
the delights of spreading sharp practice in the market place
A lesson in taking responsibility, which featured the removal of a
wheelbarrow left outside a doorway. Demarcation disputes between
gradually descending levels of seniority got increasingly bitter, as
each person tried to pass the buck, until, to laughter and applause,
the gardener, who owned the barrow, walked on whistling, and
wheeled it away.
Several large scale musical items featured the lovely tenor voice of
Billy Henderson, a local man who had come into contact with MRA
as a result of being the window cleaner for Wolfhill House.

The scene featuring the row between husband and wife was played by
Gordon and Hilda, and their performance must have been truly realistic.
Brian who was aged about 7 at the time watched the scene and ran crying
from the room: he had never seen the two of them fighting before and
couldn't understand what was going on.

Over the first four years of the family's time in Wolfhill, there was a
constant stream of visitors who had connections with MRA and whose
duties brought them to Northern Ireland. They included men such as David
Ogilvie, a naval officer specialising in bomb disposal, Dr. Will Davey, who
joined the RAF medical branch, Michael Thwaites, an Australian soldier
poet. Others who became regulars were locally based: people such as Billy
Arnold, head of the Boilermakers Union, and his wife Ivy; Jim McCuaig, a
member of the senior management team in Harland and Wolff, and his wife
Ada; Arnold Wedgwood, one of the partners in a City garage repair
business; Tom Huston, a freelance photographer, who established a
darkroom in the house. Lionel Pennefather, an expert with Border Collies
and winner of many championships, came with his dogs. Heather
Newenham came originally to work as a land girl in the garden, which was
very productive; she later worked full-time with MRA and eventually
married Lionel. The list could go on, but those included give some idea of
the extraordinary variety of people who became totally involved with MRA,
and who were prepared to commit their lives to God's control.

1944 - Afternoon tea on the lawn - Wolfhill - Far distance Gordon and Florrie, David as waiter.

The Wolfhill team inspecting Frank Buchman's 65th Birthday album - Greetings from Belfast.

Even during the 'Battle Together For Britain' days, the training through seminars and through personal contacts continued. Gordon concentrated particularly on his contacts with men and women – both in the Trade Unions and on the management side – in the industries which were of such special importance to the war effort. He also spent time keeping up his contacts south of the Border. He carried a strong sense of responsibility for the MRA team in Dublin, who sometimes felt themselves cut off from the rest of the world by the neutrality of their country. Gordon maintained his personal relationship with Eamonn de Valera, trying always to break down the barriers of age-old distrust which continued, not only between the Irish and the English, but also between the two parts of Ireland, North and South.

In Wolfhill House itself, the permanent Team living there were always aware of the need for the regular renewal of personal commitment. With the driving force of their dedication, there was a constant pressure for the pursuit of the highest standards. The watchwords 'As I am, so is my nation', 'God has a plan for every man' and others, demanded the highest levels from those who were putting them forward. The team was being prepared for the greater challenges that would lie ahead, after the war, when many of them would find themselves working and witnessing abroad.

With an increasing number of other full-time MRA people living permanently in Wolfhill, there was a strong feeling that Gordon and Hilda's large family should have a separate establishment. Once again, Sidney Gibson, from Dublin, stepped into the breach. The house in central Dublin, which he and others had bought for the MRA team there, was sold and the funds released contributed towards buying Rathmore, in Greenisland, about seven miles from central Belfast. In November 1944, the Hannon family moved into their new home.

David Telford and his wife Panny (she and her daughter Joy both played Queen Elizabeth in the revue) had been living in the Dublin house. Now they came up to Belfast, with their three daughters, on a permanent basis, and selflessly took on the responsibility of providing the central family focus for Wolfhill.

After the war came to an end, in the late summer of 1945, Gordon was asked to go to the USA to take part in a World Conference at Mackinac *(pronounced Mackinaw)* – MRA's headquarters in America. Frank Buchman was finalising his plans for the re-building of the moral structure of Western Europe. Travel was at a premium and Gordon had to seek support from all available sources to get permission for the journey. One who stressed the importance of his going was Dr Gregg, the Archbishop of Armagh.

Gordon travelled on a cargo ship which could take just twelve passengers. He heard that three of them played Bridge, a game he really enjoyed. When the other three wanted to set the stakes, Gordon told them that he didn't gamble. His partner had enough confidence in the system that they had agreed to play to take responsibility for the results and for any financial consequences! As Gordon always loved the sea, he enjoyed the voyage and the chance to have a real rest.

The political threat from the Communist regime of the USSR was already clear to Churchill, Roosevelt and many of the emerging leaders in Western Europe. Frank Buchman recognised the magnitude of the threat; that it was a planned ideological force working on an international scale, which could only be resisted and answered by a bigger and better idea. Fascism in all its forms had been seen to be a disaster, but when it collapsed, many people who had lived under its regimes were left with an ideological vacuum in their hearts.

Everyone knows that 'Nature abhors a vacuum'. Buchman had recognised the need and was setting about organising an ideological answer to be ready to enter the battle for the minds of men. This answer would be carried by a team of men and women, fully trained and driven by their total dedication to delivering God's plan. This was the reason for Gordon's call to go to the States to be part of that force.

When the War broke out in 1939, a large international team was working with Frank Buchman in the USA. Among them were several Britons, including Bunny Austin, the brilliant tennis player who had helped Great Britain to win the Davis Cup. There were also men and women from South Africa; Gordon made particular friends with Bremer Hofmeyr and his wife Agnes.

In the early days of the war, a vicious smear campaign was waged in the British press against the British men, accusing them of cowardice and draft dodging. Tom Driberg, a Labour MP and a journalist, who was a long-time bitter opponent of the Oxford Group, was the principal author of these articles which completely ignored the fact that the people concerned had travelled to the States with the permission of three different British government departments. Peter Howard, a former English Rugby captain, who had been a star fellow-journalist on Beaverbrook's Daily Express, wrote a book called 'Innocent Men' rebutting Driberg's allegations. *(Many years later, Howard was to succeed Frank Buchman as leader of the MRA movement after Buchman's death in 1961.)*

It is worth noting that most of those British men joined the American forces after the USA came into the War in 1941, although Bunny Austin was turned down after failing his medical, as he was found to be suffering from a periodic liver malfunction. Nearly all of them were given priority release from the services immediately the War ended, and they were back with the team by the time Gordon arrived.

In November 1945, Gordon sent a report from America to the Archbishop of Armagh. What follows is a series of extracts from a long and detailed letter.

"As we reach the climax of the World Assembly for Moral Re-Armament, I want to give you some impressions which seem to me most significant for the Church and for the life of our country.

"I have met delegations from many countries – twenty in all have been here this summer. Holland sent a team of six – four Protestants and two Roman Catholics, including Father Fritz van der Meer, who comes with a mandate from his Bishop and the Archbishop of Utrecht to study us as a force. His time here has been one of the most significant things for me. He came as an intellectual, a Catholic of Catholics. He witnessed to us about the change that has taken place here and how necessary it was – he spoke of the ecclesiastical pride that had gripped him, his pride of intellect, the intellectual comfort of a beautiful system. 'Truth,' he said, 'may at times divide, but Charity always unites. If all the Protestants in Holland had this kind of love for us Catholics, and if all of us Catholics had this love for the Protestants, the unity of the churches would be a reality.'

"Everyone experiences here the atomic force of the Holy Spirit in a fighting fellowship taking responsibility for a world battle. A new openness of heart has opened up new steps for me and has thrown new light on many of our Irish problems. It is alarming how in Ireland we have kept fighting on false battle-lines, and how indeed fear has turned this into national policy.

"A distinctive weapon that has been developing, has been our new plays. 'The Forgotten Factor' is an industrial play dealing with labour-management relations and emphasising the influence of home life on both labour and management. It was shown to a great audience in Washington under the joint chairmanship of President (then Senator) Truman and Congressman Wadsworth. Members of the MRA team have visited the homes of 2000 union leaders. During the War, the battle over here was for production; now it is definitely for control. The Marxist forces are using every weapon to grip the minds of American workers.

"Someone has described this year's World Assembly as 'the Headquarters of the Hope of the World'. I think this whole united force will eventually move into Europe. I hope they will touch Ireland on the way. The teams visiting here have been facing the cost of laying the foundations for world re-making.

"I hope we shall be faithful enough to get the right Irish leadership, North and South, to this European Assembly when it takes place. To translate the miracles of Mackinac into terms of Irish life gives me a vision of Ireland providing the world with the answer to many problems. I have seen the answer worked out here to the following:

1. The destiny of small nations
2. The answer for minorities
3. How an over-arching ideology can unite conflicting interests and eliminate divisive points of view
4. A Christian philosophy of Industry

"I am specially grateful for renewed contact with Dr. Frank Buchman. He is undoubtedly a man with prophetic vision.

"Dr. John R. Steelman, who has just been appointed President Truman's personal adviser, described the MRA forces as the greatest single force in the nation for reconciliation. A great triumph has been the public recognition of the value of MRA-trained forces by a direction issued from the highest quarters for their immediate release from the American army, because they were needed 'for the national safety'.

"I realise the great reserves of Christian experience we have in Ireland. My thoughts have been going back to 1918, at the beginning of my ministry. We drifted then, in spite of our keenness, because the issues were not clear in our own personal living. 1945, in a sense, holds greater potentialities for drift and disaster, but there is also, in the hearts of multitudes, what President Truman describes as 'A hunger for great living'. There is also this one outstanding difference – the fact of MRA, a trained force, thousands strong, on the march together under the direction and in the life-giving power of the Holy Spirit.

"I have written fully what is in my heart as I feel a strong sense of responsibility to report on the proceedings here. I know your sincere interest, and I am grateful for your sympathy and help since College days right up to now."

Shortly after Gordon returned from America, Leslie was de-mobbed from the RAF. Leslie tells an interesting story about Florrie Dowds. She told him that Hilda had thought that Michael's birth, on the same day as Leslie had gone to join up, meant that while she had 'lost' one son, she had gained another. Hilda had held onto this strange concept until the day she saw Leslie walking up the long avenue at Wolfhill in all the glory of his de-mob suit! Florrie was a truly remarkable person. She kept her finger on the pulse of the whole family. She was the one person everyone knew would listen to any troubles that arose.

Leslie's return meant that the whole family, Gordon, Hilda, the six children and Florrie were at home and settled in Rathmore.

Interlude For Reflection

At this stage of the story it is perhaps worth while stepping back for a moment and assessing what had happened to Gordon's vision, which we first met in his speech as a graduate divinity student to the T.C.D. Theological Society in 1915 (*see pp 17&18*). Even then he was thinking on a global scale.

After Trinity, his total concentration was on his work in the Church of Ireland. He was always ready to face a challenge – as when he took on the responsibility for the Trinity College Mission in Belfast. He also had the extra ability that enabled him to identify problem areas, and the self-confidence to have the courage to tackle them head on.

The same self-confidence and courage were both fully stretched when he moved, in succession, first to Ballymoney (itself a big enough parish to require a curate) and then on to deal with the enormous demands of Lurgan. His vision was always to make his parish operate, as nearly as possible, to its fullest potential, both in terms of faithfulness and worship to the Glory of God, and in witness to that Glory by its work among the community. The vision was still within the confines of his dearly loved Church of Ireland.

When he was challenged by his early contacts with the Oxford Group, he was asked to take a close look at himself, and at what was driving him. By his own writings we can see that, while he certainly had had the good of his beloved Church very much at heart, he was also pleased and possibly self-satisfied by his achievements up to that stage. Now he was being challenged to widen his horizons and to begin to think in terms of the country as a whole. He was being asked to realise that spreading the idea of total dedication to God's guidance was an answer that would be worth while for every man and woman in every place.

Gordon took this very much to heart on a personal basis and, at the same time, he was ready to pass on similar challenges to those he worked with – beginning with his own family relationships and with friends and colleagues in Lurgan. Notes from his sermons written in the 1930's clearly illustrate his determination to set the same high standards to his congregations as he was demanding of himself.

The visit to the United States and Canada was his first opportunity to get a taste of what it meant to be part of a movement which was prepared to operate on an even wider scale.

By 1938/39, the imminence of war, and the inspiration of working closely with Frank Buchman, led directly to the decision to dedicate himself to the concept of working full-time as part of the international Moral Re-Armament movement. Restrictions on travel during the war years meant that most of his work was done within the confines of the island of Ireland. This in itself meant that he had the opportunity of sharpening his insights in dealing with the traditional problems of his homeland.

His commitment to the war effort in the North involved him in the whole area of industrial relations, where he found himself faced with the realities of a global ideological struggle for the hearts and minds of men and women from many different backgrounds. These were men and women with fire in their bellies and passion in their beliefs. At the same time, his contacts with men and women in the South were often with people in positions of leadership and responsibility whose convictions were, in many cases, the product of centuries of understandable bitterness. They had no less fire and no less passion. The challenge always was to convince people, in all these situations, that there was a greater driving force available.

Working with them gave Gordon just the experience he needed most when the war ended, and he found himself working in wider fields. When he came back from the USA in 1946 he knew that the great battle-lines had been firmly drawn, and that a new struggle was about to take off for the soul of Europe.

Rathmore and Overseas

Although the family moved into Rathmore in the winter of 1944, Gordon continued to lead the work of the team based in Wolfhill.

After he returned from the USA the pressure was on to prepare for the arrival of Frank Buchman's international team who were bringing 'The Forgotten Factor' to Europe. Although Buchman's team actually sailed into Southampton on the Queen Mary, the decision was taken that the first European staging of the play would be in Belfast. The opening night was 17th June 1946.

On the evening before, Gordon was invited by Dean Cyril Elliot to preach in Belfast Cathedral. In the course of his sermon he said,

"Democracy – and by that I mean not merely a political system, but the Christian way of life we have professed belief in – is in greater danger than in 1939."

"We often talk about Ireland's part in early Christian centuries – how this country was the bridgehead of the Christian advance into Europe. The question is – have we an answer to the mighty, indignant, anti-Christian ideas that are on the march to seize control?

"Men, almost desperate for an answer say,
'We know what Berlin stood for'
'We know what Moscow stands for'
'What about Washington or London?'

"We may add, what about Ulster? The time has come for men to proclaim, with authentic voice, that our priority is not Race first, nor Class first, nor State first, nor money, nor sex, - but God first.

"We live in an ideological age. The world awaits our answer. We want the answer to the colossal selfishness of the top dog and to the colossal bitterness of the under dog. – and to the apathy and frustration of the ordinary people who stand back and watch the dog fight."

After reflecting on his experiences during his visit to the USA, Gordon spoke of the evidence of the power of the effect of 'The Forgotten Factor' on those who would go to see the play:

"I believe that teamwork already begun in homes and factories will spring to new life. The battle line of the Christian forces will be revealed and who and where the enemy is – he will be found in unexpected places.

"What is the secret of 'The Forgotten Factor', that has transformed some of the most difficult industrial situations, that inspires men to a fighting faith?

"It dramatises, in settings with which ordinary men and women are familiar, the simple foundations of Christian Democracy, Sound Homes, Teamwork in Industry and Unity in the Nation.

"What are the simple ingredients of the Christian answer?
"This is what the Trinity means to me today:
1. One absolute authority. One who cares. Who has a plan. God the Father.
2. The power to change, to have a different kind of life. Man is offered the stature of a new creature in Christ.
3. The power to live together; in the fellowship of the Holy Spirit.

"This may sound simple but it is not easy. It doesn't come easy to realise that
1. Human wisdom is bankrupt. I can so easily be Mr Know-All. It is so much easier to be the man with the answer rather than the man who is part of God's answer.
2. Absolute Moral Standards are the key to the service of God.
3. The Fact of God's Guidance. Where God guides, men are filled with His Spirit.
4. Inspired teamwork – working on the whole basis of making the other fellow great.

Gordon and Hilda with Frank Buchman at St. Anne's Cathedral Belfast 16th June 1946

"Democracy must capture and live its inspired Christian ideology, or it will become a dead No-Man's-Land between the Isms of Right or Left."

Gordon ended with a ringing challenge
"Change, Unite, Fight.

"Democracy's answering ideology meant for me that I must change – Will you?'

"Homes that pull together, pull the nation together. Has your home the answer to dictatorship – the answer to the broken homes of this land? We all believe in change for the other fellow! – Will *you* change?

"Are you creating teamwork in your job? – the inspired revolutionary teamwork that will capture the imagination of the Manager or the Trade Union Official?

"Are the forces being created that can change this city?   The way is change – simple but not easy – the signpost is the Cross.

"My vision today is this – Ulster the Bridgehead of a world re-made under God – Sound homes, Teamwork on the Job, Nations United. Where all men are free and equal to change, unite and fight for a future that is responsible and free."

Demand was so great that The Forgotten Factor played to packed houses for two weeks and Frank Buchman was there together with his team, in support of the cast, to meet the audiences, to listen to their responses to what they had seen and to make sure that their reactions were picked up and their concerns taken in hand. This follow-up of the play was a pattern followed in future years when it and other productions were staged in many different parts of the world.

While Buchman and his team were moving around Britain, hectic preparations were going on in Switzerland to establish a centre where people from other parts of Europe could come together to meet the challenges of this ideological crusade.

People from Switzerland had attended the Mackinac Conference in 1945. When they returned home they inspired a group of families with the idea that a major conference centre was needed for the work of MRA in Europe. By sacrificial giving they were able to buy an old hotel at Caux in the mountains above Montreux. The building had been about to be pulled down.

However the Swiss team were convinced it was the right place and once the purchase was complete, a small army of volunteers moved in to restore it to a condition where it could be used. International delegations were already there when Frank Buchman arrived. As he looked round at all the beaming, welcoming faces, Swiss, French, Scandinavian, British, American and so many others, he is famously remembered for his first words.

"Where are the Germans?"

This was a quantum leap for the minds of those who heard the question. However, once its full implication and the total necessity of answering its challenge had been accepted, strenuous efforts led to the arrival of the first German delegation some few weeks later.

Gordon went out to Caux almost immediately and some weeks later, in August, Hilda, Peter and I accompanied by several of the Irish team followed.

It was an extraordinary experience for a 16-year-old boy from Ulster. Beginning with the long journey across England and through a France which was still visibly suffering the physical after-effects of the War. Then arriving at Mountain House, a stunning place in brilliant summer sunshine. The old luxury hotel still maintained much of its grandeur, but it was kept running by the people who went there to take part in the Conference.

Peter and I were both involved in household care. I still have memories of the fun to be had from racing along great corridors gathering linen to be dumped into chutes from the upper bedroom floors down to the laundry rooms below and of the drudgery of an evening spent trying to clean the remains of oven-cooked 'fried eggs' from steel serving dishes. Three hours up to my elbows in grungy washing-up water!

Of course there were the other incredible moments. Sitting in the main conference hall, listening to French men and women apologising to the Germans for their bitterness, and to Germans apologising for the havoc wrought by their nation. Often there would be tears in many eyes as these extraordinary examples of pleas for forgiveness and of forgiveness openly given took place in front of us.

There were the wonderful plays. 'The Forgotten Factor' was probably the most ideologically challenging, but 'And Still They Fight', the story of the Norwegian journalist Freddie Ramm, who had been through the atrocities of torture by the Gestapo, was the most emotionally gut-wrenching.

In that immediate post-war year we experienced for the first time the delightful flavours of fresh croissants and black-cherry jam for breakfast and the astonishing taste of meat cooked in a wine-vinegar court bouillon. There were the unfamiliar sounds of constant cow-bells, and the haunting echoes of the hooting horns of cars making their way round the tortuous S-bends of the road up the mountain. There was the strange adventure of the funicular railway down from Glion on the way to the Château de Chillon. There was swimming in the warm waters of Lake Geneva and even a rowing-boat visit to Queen Victoria's wedding present from the Swiss people – a tiny artificial island in the middle of the lake.

What a setting! What experiences for 1940's Irish teenagers! But those were only the superficial wonders of the place. Throughout the months from July to September people came from all parts of Europe on the Western side of the Iron Curtain. Scandinavians, British, Irish, Italians, Dutch, Danes, Belgians, French *and Germans* all joined in with stories to tell, with messages of reconciliation to deliver, many with lessons to learn. It was an awe-inspiring time and something completely new in the post-war world.

There were so many life-changing influences to be encountered and so many life-changing challenges to be faced in the extraordinary atmosphere of the place, that, even to the present day one of the aims of MRA workers in different parts of the world has been to try to get people to Caux! In so many cases where men or women are facing personal challenges, they find themselves inhibited in making final decisions by the claustrophobic influences of the individual world they live in at home.

When they get to Caux, they find the limitations of their personal worlds shattered by the magnitude of the vision or paralleled by the experiences of others from totally different backgrounds, cultures and creeds. They can see the unlimited application of the simple assurance that God has a plan for every one. The challenge is to listen out for it, and, when it is heard, to put it into action.

For the next seven or eight years Gordon and Hilda invariably spent some time in the summer months at Caux. But the time has come to return to the chronological story.

* * * * *

Rathmore needed much work done to it, in the house itself, in the gardens, which were seriously overgrown, and in the various outbuildings where, as usual, Hilda kept a cow and raised chickens. From her inheritance from her father there was enough money to make it possible to employ Albert Kernaghan who lived in a gate-lodge belonging to the house. He was part-time gardener, cow-man, and general handyman. His presence in the set-up made keeping the livestock possible.

An altogether much more significant person, in fact the most important person in the house, and with the family, was the truly remarkable Florrie Dowds. Without her it would not have been possible for Gordon and Hilda to undertake all that they did over the next eight years.

Florrie had originally joined the family in 1936 to look after Brian. When the family moved to Wolfhill, Florrie came with us, knowing full well the basis on which the decision had been taken. She herself had accepted the concept of living under God's guidance and following his plan for her life.

Although she had left school at the usual early age of the times, she was a person of enormous wisdom which was matched only by the love and care she had for each and all of us. She was blessed with an amazing mixture of self-confidence and common sense and was never afraid to bring any of us back to basics when she saw us wandering off line.

Brian tells a story which illustrates perfectly what I am trying to describe. He writes, "Florrie became a second mother to me, and lived with us from my birth until after I left home as an adult. The relationship is summed up for me in just one tiny moment. As a young teenager, I came into the house and pulled the door shut behind me. 'Who's that?' called Florrie from upstairs, and I called back 'It's only me!' Florrie came down, sat me on a kitchen chair, and said, kindly but firmly, 'Brian, don't you ever say that again.' I was surprised and asked, 'Say what?' 'It's only me,' said Florrie. 'Don't ever say "It's only me," because you are as much loved by God and by me as anyone else in the whole wide world.' I don't believe our family home could have been the same without Florrie Dowds."

When Gordon and Hilda were away from home, which happened frequently over those next years, Florrie took charge of running the house and maintaining the home.

Leslie, back from the Air Force, went back to Queen's to complete his engineering degree. In between times, he worked with Albert Kernaghan and another local man, known to us as 'the Machine' because of his work-rate, to build a remarkable tennis hard court. The foundations were the rubble of demolished air-raid shelters covered by layers of coke clinker from the gas works, then coke, then coke dust and finally a topping of red brick-dust from the local brickworks. The fencing was completed using iron poles pulled out from a long-established hedge and great rolls of army-surplus wire netting. The total cost of this remarkable achievement was less than £120. But, regularly maintained by screeding and rolling, it gave Gordon and Hilda a great chance of enjoyable exercise in which all the older children joined enthusiastically during school holidays.

Hilda with Albert Kernaghan at Rathmore

Gordon enjoying the Rathmore tennis court

Florrie with Michael and Brian

During those years at the end of the war and just after it, Gordon worked hard with Bob Getgood. Bob was interested and involved in MRA, but at that stage he had regular battles with his own deeply rooted convictions about the rights of his people. He was still both a Member of Parliament for the Northern Ireland Labour Party at Stormont and a senior member of the Transport and General Workers Union. Not too many of his colleagues in the Union world were entirely happy with his involvement in MRA. This put him under constant pressure and Gordon, in his own words, fought for him on a regular basis. He was not always helped by the family.

On one occasion Bob came to Rathmore for an evening meal, and as usual the conversation flew back and forth across the table. All was well until, with all the wisdom of my 16 years I put forward the idea that the only solution to continuing industrial unrest in Ulster was to have a large pool of unemployed people who would then be only too anxious to work! Bob was apoplectic! He was ready to march out of a house that could be home to someone with such thoughts. Gordon managed to calm things down, and eventually he and Bob retired to the sitting room where they continued their personal discussions.

Over the years, Gordon was seldom really angry with us in the family. He could be disappointed (why would he not have been?), but seldom really cross. However, that evening he definitely was not pleased. "You nearly lost Bob Getgood for me! Do you have any idea what that could have meant?" Those may not be the exact words, but, whatever they were, that was the sense of them.

As time passed, Bob became more and more convinced of the validity of the challenge offered by MRA. He carried his convictions and his acceptance of the whole new philosophy into his part in the national life of Northern Ireland. By 1949 he was so sure of the need to carry the message to an even larger community, that he accepted Gordon's invitation to travel with him during that winter, to the Ruhr Valley.

The MRA world force was concentrating on helping to heal the wounds of the war on the European continent and the battle was on for the leadership of the German mine-workers where there was an immensely strong and well-organised attempt by Communist party people to take control.

Gordon often told the story of a time when he visited a communist Trade Union official during his time in the Ruhr. He noticed a copy of The New Testament and one of Das Capital on the man's desk. Gordon asked why he kept them together like that. In reply, the man pointed to the Bible and said, "If men lived like that, here would be no need for the other!"

Gordon and Bob made a powerful team with the firebrand style of Bob's new Christian-based socialism striking chords in the minds of the Trades Unionists while Gordon's great depth of personal experiences carried its own conviction.

Earlier, through his work with Bob Getgood, Gordon had made contact with Saidie Patterson who has been mentioned before as the leader of the Union's industrial struggle in 1940 with the employers in the linen industry. Saidie was a devout and committed member of the Methodist Church, but, as with many members of the Labour and Trades Union movements, she tended to keep her religious convictions and her political/industrial work in separate compartments.

It was fascinating, when talking about Saidie to David Bleakley, her biographer, to hear him say that they all became aware of a new dimension to their idealism when they came in contact with Gordon.

Gordon could see no reason why this compartmentalisation should be the rule. For him, his religious beliefs were the very convictions on which he had decided to base the entirety of his own life, and when he met other people with driving convictions of their own, he brought this concept of totality as a challenge.

Gordon's approach to people of conviction was never to say "You're wrong!". What he did offer was the opportunity of considering a wider vision. He brought this challenge to all people and his contacts across pre-conceived social barriers whether of class or denomination meant that people who went to Wolfhill or Rathmore – or, later, to Caux – very often found themselves sitting beside others whom they had more often seen only on the opposite side of a negotiating table, or going through a different Church door.

Suddenly they began to realise that these 'other people' were very like themselves, with human problems that were all too familiar. Problems at home, problems with children, problems with money, personal jealousies, personal problems with 'the other side' at work, problems with facing their own dishonesty.

In his book about Saidie, David Bleakley describes how, in 1946, she made the surprising announcement that she had found her new strategy – Moral Re-Armament.

He continues "The influence of Bob Getgood was crucial. Some years earlier Bob had formed a friendship with Gordon Hannon... Fiery trade union leader and highly disciplined clergyman, they formed a remarkable partnership, and between them carried the message of MRA into every part of Ireland. After the war they concentrated on the industrial centres of the North of Ireland."

When 'The Forgotten Factor' came to Belfast, Saidie and a group of her shop stewards (incidentally, including David's wife Winnie) were among those invited.

David remembers what Saidie said about that evening: "I shall never forget that night or the questions asked when it ended. They were new to me and they worried me because they seemed too fundamental to ignore.

"They were going on about Ireland's role in the revival of post-war Europe... They believed, and asked us to believe, that Ulster could be a pioneer again for a Christian way of living for the whole world. They talked about an ideology above party, class or viewpoint, offering to people everywhere a place in the front line."

Later, when Saidie and some of her colleagues were invited to visit Caux, it was to prove a watershed, affecting the rest of her career. She had found her 'new dimension'. Some of her friends thought she had 'gone soft'.

As David reports, "a criticism, which Saidie often said, with a glint in her eye, 'that they were careful not to repeat in my presence'."

At Caux, Saidie's first contribution was a typical 'back to the barricades' speech trouncing the industrialists in the audience as she re-told a good deal of the industrial history of the Shankill Road. When she met Frank Buchman the next day he remarked "I gather from your speech yesterday that you weren't too keen on the bosses".

Saidie launched into another attack on reactionary management. Buchman listened and then asked "Well, suppose I gave you all the weapons you needed and suppose all your hard men were destroyed and gone – where do we go from there? Do you really believe that class hatred is the answer? When you're filled with it, where does it get you?"

Thinking over all these things, and experiencing the full impact of events in Caux, Saidie came home firmly and irrevocably committed to MRA as the answer for her future life. She continued with her work with the Trade Union and as a leading member of the Northern Ireland Labour Party and became a regular visitor to Gordon's home. Looking back later, Saidie often said that she achieved more for her girls by applying absolute moral standards, and by working for 'what' not 'who' was right, rather than by using the old methods of confrontation at the negotiating table.

A very interesting sidelight on the impact that MRA was to have on industrial relations comes from further correspondence from Sir Graham Larmor. In July 1953 he wrote to Gordon. At the time, Bob Getgood and Saidie had been part of a Trade Union delegation who were meeting with the Linen Trade Employer's Association. Bob and Saidie had plans to go to Caux that year. Larmor wrote, "The position was (until a week ago) that negotiation was the basis for a settlement. We thought we had this at a good level but unfortunately it broke down just a few days after Mr. Getgood and Miss Patterson left so abruptly.

"Had they remained in Belfast I believe that their influence would have been the determining factor. Their absence meant that a person believed to be "C"[*ommunist*]-minded was more or less left in command and as a result the decision went the wrong way. Now our Industry has returned, sectionally, to open warfare, and some of us (including Mr. Getgood and Miss Patterson) have thrown away a month or more's work."

Referring to a senior Trade Union representative from Dublin, Larmor's letter continued "Lack of support from N.I. Trade Union people probably resulted in his giving in to the majority in Belfast who wished 'warfare' rather than negotiation. Again, to be fair, I must say that some of our fellow-employers proved very difficult during the negotiations ... I told Mr Getgood on the phone, just before he left, how regrettable it was that they were both going off at that moment and he agreed entirely, but the plans had been made."

Larmor was clearly very unhappy, but it is a fascinating insight into the effects of Gordon's contacts with people on both sides of the industrial fence, that they trusted him enough to be so open with him and to confide in him when they all knew that he was working energetically with the people 'on the other side'.

Graham Larmor's correspondence with Gordon reveals a steady growth of trust between them, and an increasing awareness of the value of the work being done on the industrial scene by Moral Re-Armament. At the same time, he is determined to keep the personal decisions that he realised MRA would demand from himself at arm's length. Another letter reads "While Moral Re-Armament is not something I can identify myself with in any active manner, I do pay tribute to, and will support in various ways, its efforts on behalf of mankind and a better order."

Gordon's reply to his earlier letter makes it clear that Larmor had contributed financially to the costs involved in Bob Getgood and Saidie travelling to Caux. In his reply, Gordon writes "No doubt they will put things right about the question of being away at a critical time. I know how greatly they value the work that has been done together. It is a tough battle, but it will bear fruit."

* * * * *

Early in 1948 there was a General Election in Eire and when the votes were counted it turned out that, for the first time since 1932, Fianna Fail, Eamonn de Valera's party, did not have an overall majority. This was interpreted by all the other parties as a clear signal that the country wanted a change and as a result, in spite of their many different and disparate elements, they got together to form a coalition Government, leaving de Valera as Leader of the Opposition. In view of de Valera's commitment to the concept, it was remarkable that it was under the Coalition that 'Eire' formally and permanently became the Republic of Ireland.

Later the same year 800 delegates gathered in Holland, at the Hague, for the European Congress. The purpose of this meeting was to think ahead about the future for Europe. After experiencing the dreadful traumas of two World Wars, people were determined to do what they could to establish some concept of unity, which would be voluntary rather than the consequence of conquest.

Ireland was one of the participating countries and, although he was no longer in government, de Valera was in a position to send a delegation. He had a strong conviction that such a group of people should recognise the reality of the Protestant community in Ulster. He issued an invitation to Gordon to join him at the Hague and to bring a companion. Gordon asked his friend, Ulster Unionist M.P. Fred Thompson, to go with him.

Although there was a section of those attending the Congress who thought that the ideal solution for the future would be a complete political union somewhat parallel to the U.S.A., the clear view of the majority was that a planned series of steps recognising common cause would be wiser. This attitude resulted in the decision to set up the Council of Europe which would meet for the first time the following year in Strasbourg. From this early beginning, the process, which eventually led to the modern European Union, has steadily grown.

Gordon found the meeting at the Hague an exciting and challenging place with its opportunity for building relationships not only within the Irish delegation but also across European national boundaries.

Amongst his particular friendships were those with Ole Björn Kraft from Denmark, who later became Danish Foreign Minister and chairman of NATO, and with Eleanor Butler, who was a member of the Irish Labour Party and had been elected to the Irish Senate following the General Election. Eleanor, who later became a friend of the family, was particularly struck by the stories of what was happening at Caux. The apologies for bitterness towards Germany from Frenchwoman Irène Laure, the Secretary-General of the national organisation of socialist women, and a Member of Parliament from Marseilles; the early insistence that German industrialists, Trades Union leaders and politicians should be included. These were eye-opening reports to the young Irish Senator, who could see an immediate challenge to the bitterness and negativity often affecting Irish politics.

Both Kraft and Eleanor Butler eventually worked on a fully-committed basis with MRA and were members of the international team which Frank Buchman led to Asia in 1955.

* * * * *

By 1949 various significant changes had taken place on the family front at home in Rathmore. Leslie had completed his engineering degree at Queen's University and was working with an engineering firm in Belfast. Peter had just graduated from Oxford, where both he and I had been lucky enough to be awarded the closed Norman scholarships, for sons of Church of Ireland clergymen, from St. Columba's College in Dublin to Keble College. Ruth, whose education was being paid for by Hilda's mother ('Granny Denny' to one and all), was enjoying an outstanding career at Cheltenham Ladies College. Brian was about to start his time at St. Columba's and Michael was fast approaching life at boarding school.

During his Oxford years, Peter had made many friends from different parts of Africa – particularly from South Africa, and from the English-speaking countries of West Africa. He had made the personal decision to follow Gordon's example and commit himself fully to MRA. After graduation in 1949, he went to Caux together with Ruth, Brian and myself. When the rest of us returned home, Peter stayed on.

Silver wedding at Rathmore 11thApril 1948 taken by Leslie with Granny Denny standing between Peter and David.

That year, the decision had been taken to run what was known as 'The Good Road College' which brought together young men and women from all parts of the world who were making a commitment to MRA for ideological training and forward planning.

Although the Annual International Conference at Caux usually came to an end in September, the College ran on to early December that year. While Peter was there, Dr. Azikiwe who was Head of the National Council of Nigeria and the Cameroons, arrived in Caux and Peter was appointed as his 'ADC'.

Dr. Azikiwe had come to Britain leading a delegation to the Colonial Office to discuss a programme for independence for his country. When the idea was peremptorily dismissed by the British officials, Azikiwe was furious and was ready to accept an invitation to go, first to Prague to attend the Communist inspired Civil Rights Conference, and then on to Moscow. However an African friend invited him to visit the home of an English family who were fully committed to MRA. This was Azikiwe's first experience of a welcoming white family who were prepared to treat him as an equal and of being given an opportunity to discuss things on an equal level with white men. This experience led to his decision to cancel the visit to Prague and visit Caux instead.

Before he left to return to Nigeria, Dr. Azikiwe, later to become the first President of an independent Nigeria, spoke to the main gathering at the conference declaring that he had made the decision that for him the future of Nigeria should be decided on the basis of 'What's right' not 'Who's right'. Before he left Caux, he cabled to Obafemi Awolowu (his principal opponent) to meet him at the airport on his return. When they met, Azikiwe's new attitude led to much less bitterness and violence in future political battles.

In December 1949, Peter came home to Rathmore and, at a gathering of those who worked with Gordon and Hilda, held in Belfast in Fred Thompson's house, he spoke of his personal decision to dedicate himself to working in Africa. His friends felt that this decision demanded financial backing, and they raised the money to cover the journey. With this generous support, Peter took off for Cape Town early in 1950.

There he began a life which kept him in Africa, apart from visits to Caux and occasional visits home, for the best part of the next thirty years. During the years of full-time work with MRA, exactly as Gordon had decided in 1940, Peter had no guaranteed income and no 'job security' in the normal materialistic sense. But he was convinced that the decision he had taken was the right thing for him and that, in carrying out what he saw as God's plan for him, God would provide.

Meanwhile at home in Ireland, for the rest of us, family life continued.

* * * * *

Leslie had become very keen on Pat Smale, whose father was American Consul General in Belfast. However, when Pat's father was posted to Cape Town, the friendship had to be continued by long-distance letter writing. Leslie describes how things developed:

"When Pat's Dad was transferred to Cape Town, things between us were not that serious: I sure liked her, but she has never let me forget that I didn't go down to the boat to see her off because I had a Maths test that night! Well, we soon started writing to each other and over the next 20 months love blossomed. Finally, in a letter, I asked her to marry me – she cabled back 'Yes'. It's amazing to think that for all that time we hadn't spoken to each other – no phones, no computers, no e-mail, only letters."

By the time of Leslie's engagement, I was in my third year at Keble, with 'finals' lying in wait. Ruth had won the top scholarship to Bedford Physical Training College and was in the first year of a three-year course. Brian and Michael were well settled into St. Columba's College, Dublin and Mourne Grange, respectively.

Each summer, Gordon and Hilda spent long periods in Switzerland, working with the MRA team there, and constantly encouraging the Irish men and women they worked with at home to come out to the Annual Conference at Caux, so that they could experience the extraordinary atmosphere of the place.

In different years, various members of the family joined them there. Brian still has his 'holiday diary' for 1949 which describes the adventure with all the wonder of a 12-year-old. Interestingly, that diary mentions the fact that Gordon had attended the Council of Europe in Strasbourg that same year, where he and Senator Butler were still members of the Irish delegation.

The core team at Caux was truly international. Not only were there people from all parts of Europe and the British Isles, but there were many men and women from America, South Africa, Australia and New Zealand. In addition, as the message of MRA spread world-wide, there were increasing numbers of visitors from India and the Far East.

Gordon was always delighted to be able to team up again with the Hofmeyrs from South Africa, whom he had met in 1945 in America. They were well aware of Peter's decision to work in Africa and, in fact, he was based in the Hofmeyrs' own part of the country.

Once Leslie's proposal of marriage had been accepted, the wedding was arranged to take place in Cape Town. Gordon and Hilda were very keen to be there for the big event and it was made possible when it was agreed that they should visit South Africa and work with the MRA team there. Plans were made to travel out, together with Leslie, in March 1951 and to spend some months working in Africa before the wedding, intending to return to Europe in time for part of the Caux Conference, which was scheduled to begin, as usual, in the summer months in Switzerland.

African Adventures

Leslie had spent several months, towards the end of the War, in Rhodesia, training to be a pilot in the RAF. That particular ambition had been frustrated when it became obvious that the Allies were winning the war, and the authorities cut back on the training programme. However, the experience of Africa had stayed with him, and so he was very happy to plan to emigrate permanently. Although he had decided, on a personal basis, not to throw in his lot with MRA, he, Gordon and Hilda, travelled out together on board the Edinburgh Castle.

During the voyage, Gordon and Hilda had something of a shock when they heard that I had been involved in a car accident. On a wet Easter Monday morning I was driving into Belfast with Ronnie Williams, a friend from College, when a 37-ton fire engine drove out of a side street and hit the side of the car. By some miracle neither Ronnie nor I was seriously injured although the car was a complete wreck. When an ambulance delivered the two of us home that evening, a remarkably unflustered Florrie took control of the situation as usual, and order was restored.

Describing the arrival in South Africa, Leslie writes, "What a great day it was when we finally met again after the boat docked in Cape Town. I spent ten days staying at Tembani, the Consul General's house, with Pat and I getting to know each other again. Then I went off to Johannesburg to get a job and sort out somewhere to live."

Meanwhile Gordon and Hilda were hard at work with the local MRA team. They realised very early on the truth of what people often say: if the Irish can solve their own problems, they will have much to offer to the divided communities in other parts of the world.

During the years of World War II, most people in the United Kingdom had looked on South Africa as a part of the British Empire, led by Jan Smuts, who had loyally supported the Allied cause. Gordon and Hilda found it surprisingly different, with bitter divisions between the Afrikaans-speaking descendants of the Boers and the English-speaking community who still tended to think of Britain as the 'home country'. When they met with the

Afrikaners, Gordon and Hilda found that their own experiences of living through the years of the Civil War in the South of Ireland and the brutal sectarian violence in the North during the early '20's, allowed them to establish early friendships.

The remarkable stories coming from Caux, telling of the reconciliation between Germans and men and women from the many other European countries who had suffered at their hands, were powerful weapons in reaching the hearts of Afrikaner men and women. Perhaps what affected them most, was not the impact of the apologies from the Germans for what they had done, but rather, the power of the apologies from people such as the Frenchwoman Irène Laure, who had suffered so terribly at their hands. What was that power? It lay in the simple fact that she had realised the impossibility of building new relationships with anybody, so long as her own heart was poisoned by a personal historical bitterness.

Hilda told a moving story of a woman who had decided to give her life to God's control. When she realised that this meant giving up her life-long bitterness against the British, she went upstairs and brought down the blood-stained shirt her grandfather had been wearing when he was killed in the Boer War. She said to Gordon and Hilda that this was the symbol of her hatred, and, if the hatred had to go, the shirt had to go with it. She took the shirt and burnt it in the stove. It was an almost sacramental demonstration of total change.

There have been criticisms launched at MRA by people who had their own reasons for rejecting its challenge; that the movement was only interested in 'top people'; that there was almost an ideological snobbery in their attitude. While it is certainly true that leaders and people of influence were targeted, it must be said that this targeting took place at all levels – from Government to Grass-Roots; from Boardroom to Factory-Floor; from Cardinals to Parish Priests; from Union Boss to Shop Steward. It makes perfectly obvious sense to aim at the opinion-formers. If the ordinary men and women see obvious change in the leaders amongst them, they will want to know the reason why.

Gordon was invited to be a keynote speaker, twice in Bulawayo and, later, twice in one day in Salisbury. His personal notebook contains the outlines of each of the addresses, which obviously have many common themes. The earliest was given when he was invited to preach in Bulawayo Methodist Church and the following excerpts, expanding on his notes, should give a clear flavour of much of what he said.

He began by describing Christ's commission to his Disciples giving them 'All Power, for All Nations, over All Things, for Always'. He stressed the amazing fact of how, in just three years, Jesus trained twelve men who were then able to turn the course of history.

He asked the question "Can anything be done today?", and went on to say that no thinking person could be unconcerned by a world situation which appeared to offer an uneasy Cold War truce in Europe, the Korean War in the Far East, and the rumblings of revolution in Africa.

He compared the two 'Camps' fighting for the future of the world.

In the first Camp were those, like International Communism, who believed that the solution to world problems was to be found by 'Changing the System'. These were people who had no place for God, but could be seen to rule by the dictatorship of fear in their organisation of materialism.

In the second Camp – the Camp of true Christianity – men and women believed the alternative revolutionary concept that 'Human Nature can be Changed?'. They know that change is essential – social, economic, political, industrial, national – but this can only stem from change within man himself on a colossal scale.

Between the two Camps, Gordon described those he referred to as 'the Misty Millions' - reluctant men and women, unwilling to make decisions, and often drifting, by the default of conviction, into the temptations of materialism. The knowledge of these temptations was something fully understood by the ideologies from the first Camp.

Gordon went on to stress how people who avoided facing up to Christ's total challenge could often be found promoting division between Churches, and, indeed, divisions within Churches; people exploiting self-will and self-importance and those personal resentments and imagined personal slights that can so easily sabotage Christian work.

After defining this concept of the two Camps battling for the hearts and minds of the Misty Millions, Gordon offered the challenge of a truly Christian ideology, MRA, promoting a universal message and a world strategy; a world family and a force committed under God's guidance to re-making the world. He spoke of how he had asked himself the question "How can I be part of this?" and he went on to describe the personal challenges he had had to face; how his very 'success' in human terms in his work in Church Ministry had blocked the Almighty Power of God.

He had found himself forced to face the need for 'Change in Me; Change in My Family; Change in My Church'.

Challenging his audience with the new rallying-cry 'Not Who's right, but What's right', Gordon stressed the needs, demands and values of the four Absolute Standards and the questions they posed. For example, under the heading 'Absolute Unselfishness' he asked:

"What am I guided by?
"Am I seeking to do God's Work in my way or to do God's Will in His Way?"

He believed that just as many people were kept from doing God's work of 're-making the world' by 'good' things as by bad things, because such people had not accepted the double commitment of combining God's Will with God's Way.

The final challenge Gordon gave in that sermon was to issue the invitation of a Christian ideology: "Come and join in 're-making the world' by putting your life under the total control of God. Learn to be guided by God in everything. Come and lead a new kind of life.

"Let the Almighty Power of God into action in your life. Take on a new dimension and become part of the greatest revolution of all time when the Cross of Christ transforms the world."

After their time in Rhodesia, Gordon and Hilda went back to South Africa.

Following after any tour of 'The Forgotten Factor', there were always people with questions to be answered. The play would have challenged them about job-related problems, about human, personal and family problems and, perhaps most significantly, about the way in which these things are inextricably linked. These challenges sounded echoes in the minds of thousands of those who heard them. The job of the team was to be there to help people who were saying, "Yes, I understand; yes, I get the message, but what do I do next?"

These constant demands could not be just brushed off or satisfied with an instant short-hand response. They needed careful attention and a support plan. The travelling team members had to be sure that they worked in close co-operation with the local folk, to make sure that men or women who were actively seeking God's answer to personal, workplace, political or other problems, were not given a simple quick palliative response. It was hard, demanding work built into a hectic peripatetic programme.

* * * * *

Shortly before leaving for home, Gordon and Hilda had the great joy of being in Cape Town on June 1st 1951 for Leslie and Pat's wedding. What made the day even more wonderful for them was the fact that Dr. Donges, the Minister of the Interior in South Africa had made Gordon a Marriage Officer for the one day so that he could marry his son and his new daughter-in-law in St Saviour's Church in Claremont.

Once again Gordon's notebook holds the details of what he planned to say in his address during the service. It is interesting to see how he built the challenge he, himself, lived by into what he said on this so much smaller 'domestic' setting. Again some quotations – this time in note form.

Leslie and Pat's wedding in Cape Town. L-R Mr and Mrs Smale, Les and Pat, Peter (Best Man)
Pat's sister Mary (Matron of Honour), Bridesmaids Amy and Juanita, Hilda and Gordon.

Les and Pat – both home builders
High hopes. Determined to make a success
Friends across the world are with you
This is a small fraction of what is in the heart of God for you
Never imagine you need to persuade God to give you things. He is
1000% ready. More than we can ask or think.
God has a Plan – but he is dependant on us to work it out
The significance of Wedding in Church 1.Legal 2. Religious
The great gift of human love is God's gift. The Power to give it fully
to each other and to be kept from confusing love with self-love
comes from Him.
Together you lay His gift on His Altar
One of the great secrets of life – GOD FIRST – even before
each other
Made one – which one?!!
Not *my* way, not *thy* way – God's way for us together
Not who is right but what is right
Home building depends on that as does Nation Building
Absolute standards bring a new security between husband and
wife – between parents and children
You will build on a foundation that will not shift
No secrets from each other
Home-building is a science
Magazines suggest gadgets and brilliant planning
What you want is a House with a Home inside it
Life ceases to be life unless there is growth
True life is growth into the plan of God
In God's world, the best is yet to be.

Shortly after returning from that first visit to Africa, Gordon and Hilda
went to the Annual Conference at Caux, taking Ruth with them. She had just
completed her first year at Bedford.

While they were there, several different plays were being staged
including 'The Forgotten Factor'. The girl playing one of the juvenile leads
was taken ill and, at very short notice, Ruth was asked to take on the part.

This she did with a remarkable fearlessness and it soon became clear that she was a first class actress. She found herself faced with a major personal decision. When she was given the opportunity of taking over the part on a full-time basis, she had to decide whether or not to take up the challenge. This would mean interrupting her course at Bedford and therefore giving up the Scholarship which she had won. She made the decision to go for it. This was a venture in faith which was fully backed by Gordon and Hilda and by other friends who gave what they could to support her.

Ruth remembers, "The first adventure was to travel with about 60 people the length and breadth of Britain, mostly in industrial areas such as London Docks, Welsh coal fields, the steel industry in Sheffield and Rotherham, the cities of Liverpool and Glasgow and the shipyards on the Clyde. We took 'The Forgotten Factor' with us. In the Green Room, before the performance of the play, people from the area would fill us in on the particular problems and potential of each place we were in so that we could meet and talk meaningfully with folk in the audience afterwards."

By 1952, the main centre of MRA activity in Northern Ireland at Wolfhill had closed down. Most of the men and women who had lived and worked there had taken their training to help with situations in many different parts of the world. Amongst the many who had spent time at Wolfhill, Bill Page and his sister Dorothy were in South Africa, Eric Turpin was working with Union leaders in the London docks (he later worked in New York), Dr. Roddy Evans was in India, Dick Laughlin was in London, as was Dr. Lance Montgomery. Lance's sister Kathleen was part of a team working in Germany, Bill Porter who had married Muriel Barrett had gone with her to Italy.

Ellie Uprichard, whose family were stalwarts of Shankill Parish in Lurgan, used all her background of the shop floor in the linen industry to spend several years with the textile workers of Northern France and later with the families of dock-workers and Trade Unionists in London and the Midlands. Dr. Ken Stewart spent four years in Italy and also worked in France. David Telford used his accountancy skills for four years with the MRA headquarters in London before later recognising a vocation to the ministry of the Church of Ireland.

Many of these men and women were the fruits of Gordon's decision taken in 1939. Now the talents of people with their level of ideological training, and personal convictions of God's purpose for their lives, were needed urgently in the many places where the battles for the souls and minds of countries were at their fiercest.

In the summer of 1952 Gordon and Hilda once again went to Caux, where Ruth was still playing her major part in 'The Forgotten Factor'. Ruth describes how, one day, the three of them were standing talking together when Frank Buchman walked along. He looked at Gordon and Hilda and said, "I hope you won't mind if I take your daughter to India!"

Buchman had received an invitation from men who had been to Caux in earlier years, asking him to bring a team to their country. His instant response was not only to say 'Yes', but to announce to his startled close friends that they would take five(!) of the plays with them.

In his official biography 'Frank Buchman – a life'*, Garth Lean describes how, sometimes Buchman would leap into making instant decisions which had to be adjusted for practical reasons. Many times, as with the question 'Where are the Germans?' which he asked at Caux in 1946, his reactions were triggered by an instant awareness of a challenge missed. Now, with the invitation to India, his immediate positive response was obviously right, but the scale had to be modified. In the end, three plays including 'The Forgotten Factor', were taken to Ceylon and India.

Ruth was part of the group of some 200 people who went on that amazing tour. Looking back, she describes what they experienced. "India was at the heart of that year of travelling, first to Ceylon and at the end of the journey to Kashmir and Pakistan. These were marvellous countries, with a wonderful variety of warmth and colour, but they had been through colossal trauma, both before and after independence. We were a kaleidoscope of largely Western people from every class and background. We were living on the basis of 'appreciation' of these Eastern lands and their people and the message of hope we brought was the acceptance of personal change and responsibility for society, first of all starting with the needs of

'Frank Buchman – a Life' published by Fount Paperback; isbn 0-00-627240-1; obtainable at www.iofc.org

our own Western countries and situations."

Ruth stayed with the group for a year including the time when they had come back to Europe in 1953. At this stage, because the productions were in French and Italian, her job was as part of the backstage team.

Eventually, after a three-year break, she returned home and completed her teacher training at the Ulster College of Physical Education. She then pursued her originally chosen career, teaching in Northern Ireland and including a period as a Lecturer at Stranmillis College of Education in Belfast. Later, she moved to London to work as Head of the Girls' P.E. Department in an enormous Comprehensive School. As well as the challenges which she faced in teaching, she also engaged in committee work with the Ulster Teachers' Union and later the N.U.T. in England. As Ruth remembers, "Many battles were fought, but I enjoyed the comradeship of the profession and found great strength from my personal commitment."

Towards the end of 1952, it was decided to send a new team to South Africa and Rhodesia. For many of the group, most of whom were younger than Gordon and Hilda, this would be a totally new experience. For Gordon and Hilda it was an opportunity to re-visit old friends and to help guide the enthusiasms of their younger colleagues.

As had happened on their previous visit, everywhere the group went they were made welcome to stay in private homes. In those years, during and after the war, critics of MRA used to ask the question "Where does the money come from?" The question was designed to imply that there were some sinister forces plotting behind the scenes to try to grab control.

The truth of the matter was very straightforward. The money came from generous, often sacrificial, giving. Earlier, Sydney Gibson's remarkable generosity has already been mentioned. In South Africa and in Northern and Southern Rhodesia, the travellers were always welcomed into homes and, on many occasions their hosts would offer to help with travelling costs to the next destination.

Among the many whom Gordon and Hilda got to know well were Rev. George Daneel and his wife Joey. Daneel was Dominee of the Dutch Reformed Church in Grahamstown and, as a former Springbok rugby player was well known throughout South Africa. He had first been in contact with the Oxford Group (as it then was) in the 1930's.

One of the purposes of the second visit made in 1953 was to hold a multi-racial conference in Lusaka, Northern Rhodesia. The Daneels took leave from their church to travel with the Hannons. This was to be a turning point in Daneel's life. At the conference he got to know Dr. William Nkomo, first President of the militantly anti-white African National Congress Youth League.

Nkomo told Daneel "I swore to drive the white man into the sea. But here I have seen white men change, and black men change, and I decided to change." He realised that bitterness had been limiting his vision and distorting his fight.

Daneel's response was "It has been the arrogance of white men like me which has caused the bitterness in men such as you."

A few months later the two men spoke side by side at a large public gathering in Cape Town's City Hall. 'The Cape Times' headlined their report of the event "Black, White on MRA Platform".

This was ground-breaking stuff for South Africa and as these men began courageously to work together – often in the face of deep suspicion from men and women of their own different backgrounds – they were among those who were to start building a pattern for the new South Africa that would eventually emerge.

Daneel, himself, spoke out fearlessly to the Synod of the Dutch Reformed Church, challenging the long-time ingrained attitudes of racial superiority and bringing them face to face with the changes in those attitudes which he knew their Christianity and Christian values demanded of them.

Daneel now began to be convinced that he was meant to work for a God-led quality of leadership, not only for his own country, but wherever he might be needed around the world. His wife, Joey, said "I knew what it would mean. There would be no fixed income, no security of home and comfort. With three small children, I could not imagine God asking a thing like that. My whole being rebelled."

Gordon and Hilda were able to share deeply about their own very similar challenges when leaving Lurgan. They were convinced that the decision facing George and Joey Daneel was indeed God's true guidance for them. They were able to demonstrate from their own experience how, once the decision was made, things had fallen into place. It had not always been easy. There had been moments when anxiety over financial or material questions had raised its head, but God had provided.

In his autobiography Daneel wrote:
"After much prayer and reflection, we were convinced that this was God's calling for us and that we should continue on the road He had shown us. There was no choice but to obey. It was God's choice, not ours. And where the future was concerned, we believed that where God guides, He provides."

Later he said "Two things especially strengthened our faith that the Lord had really called us to take the responsibility for the work of MRA. One was that the future of South Africa depended largely on reconciliation between the two racial groups. The other was that, except for the Hofmeyrs, all those taking responsibility for MRA in South Africa were foreigners, and it was essential that more of our own people should be involved."

As Gordon and Hilda continued with their travels in South Africa and the Rhodesias, the group they were with worked to a fairly regular pattern. At least half of them were still in their twenties, some from Britain, others from Scandinavia, Holland and Switzerland. In each new city they would gather each morning, when possible, to plan with interested local people what next for their public occasions and to benefit in training from the wider experience of colleagues like Gordon and Hilda.

A surviving 'Quiet Time' notebook of Hilda's from those days has been found amongst a box of old photographs. Some of the notes from her 'guidance' throw an interesting light on events.

A few examples :

"Praise God for last night: A bursting hall
                                     The Administrator of the Province
                                     The Dutch Reformed Church minister
                                     The Mayor
                                     The disciplined speakers
                                     The response of the Mayoress
                                     The music.

"Now for the next step. A lot of work to get the right new people on Monday night. Some very new voices to speak of their decisions.
"Johannesburg is a hard nut to crack. ...the Administrator should be thanked for his bold initiative. Keep checking in with him.
"The two or three who should speak to this Women's Group. What should I say? My husband's two problems – his country and his wife. ... To begin with I had no interest in being good. I put Gordon in God's place. ... Then he came home from meeting this challenge and was honest with me ... his apology. Then my fear of being honest. ...Gave him Hell for 3 months... but I saw people finding new life ... my own restitution. It is no soft or easy way ... it takes guts, depth and humility ... Is this too great a price to pay for a new heart for myself, a new home for my family, and a part in remaking my country and the world?
"If this country is ever to find its destiny, it will only be through a handful of people totally committed.
"The real joy of helping others find a new life. When I get tired or fed up, wondering what it's all about, it means, either a determination to have my own way; or covering up unhealed hurt; or protecting my fear or sense of inferiority. All reveal the deep-rooted self-centredness which has to be dealt with ... Change is not a disgrace, but a daily necessity.

Then there are thoughts that may not have been so easy to share with her husband.

"I would like to see Gordon take new steps in speaking
He has generally made fairly large, sometimes heavy speeches on
(1) The Church's function
(2) His own change
(3) The challenge of world issues
He could also be doing simple, snappy ones on
(1) Guidance
(2) Restitution
(3) Absolute Standards
"Many people here are impressed by the statesmanship of the Church of Ireland in freeing Gordon to do this work."

When they were in Northern Rhodesia, Hilda jotted down some of the national issues they would be dealing with:

(1) "Those who are blind to the tremendous force of African nationalism and determined to maintain the position of top dog and get their whack out of the country, come what may.
(2) Those who see the position clearly and are scared enough to get out while the going is good.
(3) The small group who see the obvious wrongs and injustices, who struggle hard to remove them, but without an equal struggle for a change of heart, either in themselves or other Europeans, or in the Africans on whose behalf they are struggling."

When they were in Northern Rhodesia, Gordon established a close friendship with Sir Roy Welensky, who in 1956 was to become Prime Minister of the Central African Federation. He was a remarkable man who, in his time, apart from his career in politics, had been a heavyweight boxing champion and a train-driver. The friendship carried on for many years through a regular correspondence.

After the Conference in Lusaka, Gordon and Hilda were asked to stay on to oversee the preparation and printing of a 4-page Supplement describing their campaign, for inclusion in the country's main newspaper. They were staying at the home of the Editor at the time. When Gordon became ill, Hilda had to take on the responsibility with the help of two of their younger colleagues who, like her, had little or no experience of such an undertaking!

In those parts of Africa, fresh water was often kept cool in Gordon's Gin bottles whose square shape made them easy to store. On one occasion Hilda was tired, hot and thirsty. She mixed herself a long drink of lime juice and water from the fridge, which she drank down at speed before realising to her horror that it really was gin and not water in the bottle!

In spite of such set-backs, the Supplement was completed and remained an effective tool in the hands of those carrying on the struggle, not only in the Rhodesias, but in South Africa as well.

By this time, Peter had spent some months in Kenya with a cast performing 'The Forgotten Factor'. When the play was staged in Nairobi, the audience included the Governor, sitting in the stalls, and Jomo Kenyatta, who later became first Prime Minister and then President of the country when Independence was granted in 1963, up in the balcony! After working in Kenya, Peter flew to Nigeria where he was to spend ten years.

When the time came for Gordon and Hilda to come home in 1953, they decided to break the journey, and meet up with Peter in Nigeria. Although their time there was quite short, it included some unusual experiences.

On one occasion they went, with several others, to have lunch with the Odemo of Ishara, who was Chief of an area in Western Nigeria. After the meal, the Odemo suddenly said, "My friend Peter Hannon has taught me that when man listens, God speaks. I believe all you people here do the same thing, and I would like you to help me with a very difficult problem I have with the Oba who rules the country next to me."

Hilda described in her memoirs how he told his visitors of a very serious issue, which, if left unsolved, would almost certainly lead to violence. The Odemo then handed round pens and paper and said, quite naturally, "Now let us listen to God together."

Hilda tells how they sat quietly for some time until the Odemo asked everyone what thoughts God had given them. Everyone seemed to have had the same thoughts, "The Odemo knows in his heart what is right, and God will give him the strength and humility to do it." He was very pleased that his own thoughts ran along the same lines, and in addition he had clear guidance about the actions he needed to take. Soon afterwards, the Odemo met with his neighbouring Oba, and, after he had asked for forgiveness for his attitude, the two men were able to work together in a good spirit, finding a full and satisfying answer to their problem.

Another extraordinary event illustrating the strength of Gordon's faith happened when they went for an evening meal with a Nigerian family. Suddenly there were awful sounds from the garden outside, and several of the servants came running into the house in great fear. The gardener had gone berserk and was racing around outside, brandishing a machete and threatening to kill everyone. Apparently he had been sacked and had come back seeking revenge. No one knew what to do in this weird situation.

After taking a moment to gather his thoughts, Gordon stood up and told everyone else to sit quietly. He walked over and opened the door into the garden and moved calmly towards the man who was still raving away, foaming at the mouth. As he got near to him, Gordon raised his right hand and said firmly, "In the name of Jesus Christ, I command you to come out of him". Immediately the man stopped bellowing and foaming. In a few moments he fell on his knees, with tears streaming down his face.

Hilda wrote, "I had heard of such things happening, but had never seen anything like it before. Gordon told me, as we went home that evening, that he felt certain the man was possessed and could only be cured by God."

Before going to Nigeria, Gordon had had his health problems in Rhodesia. When they reached Nigeria, Hilda found the heat and humidity practically unbearable because she was unable to sweat, which is almost a physical essential in such an equatorial climate. As a result, with both of them suffering from poor health, the decision was taken to come back quickly to Ireland – although there was no clear guidance as to what should happen next.

Second Interlude

In the early 1950's the decision was taken to close down Wolfhill House as the Headquarters for the MRA team in Northern Ireland. Most of the people who had lived and trained there had left the country and were working with national and international teams in other parts of the world.

Following this decision, Gordon and Hilda had realised that their home at Rathmore was too far from the centre of Belfast to be ideally situated to act as an operational centre for those, mostly with full-time jobs, who continued to be personally committed to work with MRA in Ulster. In 1952 the family moved to Rosemount, a large house not far from the Parliament building at Stormont.

When they came back from Africa in 1953, Gordon's health was not good. The physical strains and stresses of the previous dozen years were taking their toll, and, during the course of the year, he suffered a minor heart attack.

After a period of rest, he recovered well, but the question arose as to what the future held. Various suggestions were put forward, including the possibility of moving to England on a permanent basis, where he would find it easier and less physically stressful to maintain his contacts with other leaders at the headquarters of the main British team in London.

At the time, plans were already being made for a new international group to go to America where major ideological battles were being fought on the industrial, political and social fronts. Although Gordon had not been well, he had thought that he might have been asked to join in that venture.

However, an old friend, John Caulfeild, who was one of his closest associates, advised very strongly that Gordon should continue to live and work in Ireland. At the time there can be little doubt that Gordon was going through a period of considerable depression.

Many years later, Hilda spoke to Peter's wife Fiona of how the situation was going in those days. Fiona recalls the story:

"This was not an easy time, and Gordon must have wondered if God had any use for him. At one point, Hilda told me, Gordon threw his guidance notebook into the fire in despair. These tests are not at all unusual in men of faith."

Gordon's own notes which survive from about that time show a man determined to be totally honest with himself. In a page headed *Personal* he wrote these words:

"What I have seen.
A new conception of my own personal bankruptcy.
The need for the absolutes, black and white, and no toleration of anything less, in myself or anyone else.
In Ireland we have had woolly edges, softness – Ireland more the problem than Russia: poses a Christian standard that has been anything but absolute – in the North and even in Dublin.
I may have been little there, but that team was also my responsibility.
If I had been different, they would.
I failed at home.
My convictions were not sharp, nor clear, nor shared with conviction.
I failed with Hilda.
God has done great things for me when I let Him –
given me a new depth with Bob and the others.
'You missed the boat with management.
Too much of G.H. and too little of Me.
You organised again on a third-rate level.
Nothing will change you or Ireland except guidance and the miracles that can flow through, plus clean, clear – crystal-clear personality that I can give, and will give, and do give you here and now.' **Hallelujah!**

"Don't begin to think that you have something you can grasp as a security and passport forever.

'You must change every day and in every way because you
are dishonest, especially with yourself.
You have too many grey notes.
You wanted success, approval. Especially Hilda's.
That has often been your standard and so you sold her.
Lustful – looking for your own way and will.
You have to learn how to love.
I have given you a sacred trust in Hilda, Les, Pete, Dave, Ruth,
Brian, Mike.
Mighty material, and Pete and Ruth are taking important steps.
You've got to fight for absolute love – if you see My standard, fight for
it and I will give it. I give 100-fold in My return for every fraction
you give.
Hilda will blossom. *She* will learn *My way out* of self-will – the deep
reaches of it that are in *you too* – when you too learn My way out of all
the ambition and *pride you* have had.
Don't be afraid or reluctant to go back. If I send you, I can look after
you and your home and Ireland, or any place I send you.
You don't like to be left out (of say America).
You must always look for the best for Florrie – (thank God for her) –
and for Agnes* and Jenny*.   You have a great team.
You've got on a new basis now.
You frittered precious hours through lack of guidance.
You need to study your facts in a new way. Use them to mobilise all I'm
teaching you on principle etc. Intelligent news on each country that you
can give to others. This will be part of your change.
You have plenty of gifts – the point is they must have *God-power*
not G.H.-power or lack of it.'
Teamwork. More important to seek fellowship than get approval.
New every morning. The joy of a new day and a new way.
Fear gone like the mists.
Time for decision."

** Agnes Hartin and Jenny Boyd were two women who had given full-time commitment
to MRA, living with the family to help with the running of Rosemount in Belfast.*

Gordon's depression began to clear as he accepted the force of guidance continuing along these lines. His personal faith again took control of his living and his trust in the conviction – so clear in that long outpouring of self-examination – that God had a plan for him, was quite suddenly answered by an invitation from his old friend Dr Frederick J. Mitchell, the Bishop of Down and Dromore.

Would Gordon be interested in returning to parochial ministry with the Church of Ireland and taking on responsibility for Kilbroney Parish in Rostrevor which, at that stage, was in the Bishop's gift?

Gordon remembered that passage in his guidance,
"Don't be afraid or reluctant to go back. If I send you, I can look after you and your home and Ireland or any place I send you."

After checking the thought and the invitation with friends and colleagues in the MRA teams at home in Ireland and across in England, he and they realised that this must indeed be the plan for him which God had promised.

He accepted the invitation.

Rostrevor

"I grew up with the object of being a Parson; it never occurred to me that God had any other calling for me."

Those are the words chosen as the opening statement in this book. Gordon's early career followed that objective along a steadily rising curve. Then in 1939/1940, it became clear to him that God did indeed have another calling – one that was to take him to many different parts of the world.

Now in 1954 God was calling him back to that earlier objective. At this time there was no Archdeaconry, no Canonry. Instead there was the charge and challenge of a small rather run-down country parish. The congregation had shrunk to a small number of mainly elderly, faithful souls tied to the parish by years of tradition.

With his many years experience of effective parochial work in Ballymoney and in Lurgan, Gordon was ideally suited to the task of regeneration of the Church of Ireland family in Kilbroney Parish. It is also worth remembering that although Gordon himself was by this time 63 years old, and needed to take some care of his health, Hilda, on the other hand, was still only 51 and at the very peak of the driving physical personality which was to be the hallmark of the rest of her days.

There can be no doubt that for Gordon himself the task ahead was a challenge which brought a deep personal joy arising from facing once again the familiar routines of direct parochial responsibility. Like putting on a favourite old coat, there was a truly heart-warming feeling of a professional re-acquaintance with times past. This was no sinecure. The dilapidation existed in every field. There was a depressing spiritual apathy; the church building was in need of loving care and re-furbishment; the Vicarage itself had been allowed to fall into an almost irredeemable state of disrepair.

Kilbroney had forfeited its 'parochial status' as a result of failures on the financial front during the years preceding Gordon's appointment. Now that he was responsible for re-kindling the fires in the parish community, Gordon realised that a useful way to challenge the sluggish inertia was to make an assessment of the practical things which needed most urgent attention.

His predecessor had suffered from very poor health for many years and only occupied the Vicarage during the warm summer months. As a result, the house itself was suffering from the cumulative effects of many long years of winter's damp. One simple indication of the size of the problem could be seen in the condition of the main flooring joists under the two biggest rooms on the ground floor. It was only after Hilda's piano was set up in the drawing-room that it was spotted that the floor seemed to be moving under the load. It is no exaggeration to say that it was possible to pull handfuls of wet rotten wood from the beams underneath.

In spite of the problems, when Hilda first saw the house her heart leapt with delight. The Vicarage must be one of the most delightfully attractive rectories anywhere in the Church of Ireland. Elegantly proportioned, built in the early 19th Century and set at the foot of the slope leading to the Cloghmore Stone on the very edge of the Mourne Mountains, with every room facing south towards Carlingford Lough, the house cried out to be saved and restored to its original beauty. This was no demand for extravagance or self-indulgent folly; it was a matter of straightforward practicality.

Luckily, all of the family except Leslie and Peter were available throughout the summer months and everyone piled in to help where they could. A Parish Fête, to be held in the Vicarage grounds, was planned on a grand scale and, combined with direct giving from parishioners, raised what was then the enormous sum of £2,400. Other members of the community also contributed to the total, including Canon Boyle, the local Parish Priest, who gave Gordon a gift of money in an envelope - together with instructions not to tell any of his people!

Gordon's predecessor, Canon Gardner, had made a habit of exchanging invitations to tea with Canon Boyle, but these meetings were always kept as quiet as possible. This was never Gordon's style; in fact he had made it a priority to make personal contact with Canon Boyle soon after his arrival in

The Vicarage Rostrevor

Gordon leads Bishop F.J. Mitchell and his Chaplain Rev. Noel Mackey into Kilbroney Parish Church.

Gordon Hannon

Rostrevor. As part of his responsibilities as Vicar of Kilbroney parish, Gordon had found himself an ex officio member of the Town Committee which existed to make recommendations to the Kilkeel Rural District Council. He had been rather amused when, after he had been welcomed to the Committee by the Chairman, Rev. Victor Henderson who was the local Presbyterian minister, Canon Boyle stood up to welcome the newcomer 'on behalf of the Opposition'!

The £2,400 raised through the Fête was not only enough to cover all the immediately necessary work on the house, but there was also enough to begin dealing with some of the more urgent problems in the Church itself. Before the year was out, Bishop Mitchell agreed to restore parochial status – which Gordon felt would give a major boost to the self-confidence of the parishioners.

For obvious reasons, it was essential that Gordon should concentrate his attention on his new parochial responsibilities. However, at the same time, he was anxious not to lose contact with those he had been working with before.

Some years before his appointment to Kilbroney, the Bishops of Connor and of Down and Dromore had established what was known as the Bishops' Industrial Council for Belfast. This had certain clear limitations since it was an entirely Church of Ireland body. When it was suggested to him that Gordon might be interested in joining the Council, he came up with a broader vision and suggested instead that there should be a **Churches'** Industrial Council. This idea was approved and Gordon was appointed Chairman.

Working within this wider concept, Gordon found himself surrounded and supported by a group of people many of whom were destined to play pivotal roles in the future of the country.

Dr. Cahal Daly was a Lecturer, and later a Reader, in Scholastic Philosophy at Queen's University. From there he was appointed Bishop of Clonmacnoise, then Bishop of Down and Connor and finally Archbishop of Armagh at which stage he was elevated to membership of the College of Cardinals

Rev Sidney Callaghan represented the Methodist Church and became a very well known speaker and leader of ecumenical thought in that church of which he was elected President in 1980

David Bleakley at the time was an active member of the Northern Ireland Labour Party with strong Trade Union connections. Later he was elected as an MP at Stormont. Later again, even though he had lost his seat in the Parliament, he was invited by Brian Faulkner to join his Government – a post which he could only take up after being appointed a Privy Councillor.

Rev. Donald Frazer who represented the Presbyterian Church in those first days had trained for the ministry in Scotland and held responsibility for all the Sabbath Schools in Ireland.

Rev. John Radcliffe who ministered in Downpatrick, represented the Non-Subscribing Presbyterian Church and was their Clerk of the Synod for many years.

Others who became members of the Council at various stages included Father Michael Dallatt, who eventually succeeded Gordon as Chairman and who also later became Auxiliary Bishop of Down and Connor Diocese and Rev. Bill Boyd from the Presbyterian Church.

Cardinal Daly recalls Gordon's arrival to take up his ministry in South Down with great appreciation. He described him as showing "a prime example of reaching out across the traditional divisions of the area – and establishing a new tradition that has continued ever since." It was as a result of Gordon's work, the Cardinal says, that in South Down, since that time, ecumenism has been accepted and lived out over the years.

David Bleakley looks back on those days as a time of creating new relationships where they had notoriously failed to exist before. Bill Boyd says that Gordon's greatest achievement, arising from the work of the Council in those times was "getting Lord Brookeborough's Unionist Government to accept Trades Unionists as fellow human beings!"

As has already been suggested, Gordon and Hilda working together were a formidable team. While Gordon concentrated on re-establishing parochial functions, Hilda felt that a new spirit of involvement could be created if some practical projects involving team-work could be identified. Never one for thinking on a small scale, her first proposal was to make a new carpet for the main aisle of the church. The existing carpeting was quite threadbare.

This was a huge undertaking for the small numbers available, but when the word got round, many womenfolk from other churches volunteered to lend a hand. A visitor to Rostrevor and the surrounding country at the time would have been astonished to find women in many different houses all busily occupied in knotting heavy carpet wool onto individual square yards of backing material.

Not all were equally expert, and when the time came for the separate pieces to be joined together, some had to be sorted out and finished by Hilda's smaller team of specially strong-fingered experts. Each piece was completed by the person concerned leaving a two-inch border round the edge so that they could be joined together by the specialists. Mrs Williamson, the mother-in-law of the schoolmaster and Mrs Hutchinson the wife of the gardener at one of the bigger local houses worked with Hilda on this final stage.

When the carpet was completed, the whole thing was taken to a carpet factory in Portadown where it was professionally trimmed and finished free of charge. The owner of the factory was greatly impressed by the quality achieved, and the carpet is still wearing well in the 21st Century.

As the Vicar (or Rector) of the parish, Gordon was very aware of the proprieties necessary in his relationships with Rectors of other neighbouring churches. This led to one rather amusing situation. When visiting one of his own parishioners in Daisy Hill Hospital in Newry, Gordon realised that one of the other patients also belonged to the Church of Ireland, although not from Rostrevor. Assuming that the man's own Rector had not realised that one of his flock was in hospital, Gordon contacted his colleague to tell him.

The other Rector said that he did know about the man in question, but he had no intention of visiting the patient because they did not get on and were not on speaking terms. However he went on to say that he would be quite happy if Gordon wished to offer pastoral care any time he was back visiting the hospital. The patient had been listening to Gordon discussing parochial events in Rostrevor with his own parishioner and talking of the challenges which had to be faced. When Gordon began to speak with him in turn, he wanted to know all about the details.

Gordon described everything that was going on and said that the next major project would be to overhaul the church organ although that would be an expensive undertaking. The man asked him how much would be involved. When Gordon mentioned a figure of £400, the man said that he would be pleased to meet the costs! I don't believe that there was any spirit of one-upmanship over his clerical colleague behind Gordon's telling of this story; rather, he told it as another example of God moving in a mysterious way.

Life moved on in the parish until 1957 which was to prove the next truly eventful year. To begin with things were not good as Gordon had a series of health scares which culminated in a more serious heart attack than the one in 1953. Family memories differ as to whether this was actually a heart attack alone, or whether it also involved a minor stroke. Because of the associated high blood pressure, the consultant told Gordon that, in order to reduce it, he would have to take medication on a daily basis for the rest of his life. He was also advised that he should make as much effort as possible to cut down on the physical burdens of his parochial duties.

James Lockhart, an 80 year old parishioner, knew of Gordon's problems. He himself had retired many years earlier from working on the railways in China. When he was in his 60's he had suffered a severe heart attack which had left him so physically weakened that he could only go upstairs by taking one step at a time and then stopping to rest. After spending some years in this condition, James was advised to go to the Kingston Clinic in Edinburgh which was run on the principles of naturopathy. Following treatment there, he had found his health greatly improved - to such an extent that his particular delight now lay in walking in the Mourne Mountains. He suggested that Gordon might benefit from the same treatment.

Although Peter, in particular, and other members of the family had benefited over the years from the services of their osteopath friend Ted Dunham, Gordon thought long and hard about the suggestion James had made. He wondered what reactions might arise amongst his parishioners if they thought that he was putting his trust in what many people considered not to be proper medical practice. After much thought and prayer, and time spent seeking God's guidance in the matter, he decided that it would be the right thing to do.

The results were almost miraculous. After spending a fortnight at the Clinic, Gordon came home and kept his next appointment with the consultant who examined him and immediately wanted to know what on earth he had been doing. His blood pressure was down to normal levels and he had lost a full stone in weight. Gordon said where he had been and what he had done and, although not fully convinced, the consultant accepted that things were remarkably improved. Part of the Clinic's treatment regime involved regular exercise and Gordon was soon to be seen making his way around the town on foot.

A few months later, Gordon returned to the Clinic and Hilda went with him to study the dietary recommendations. Mr. Thompson, who was in charge of the establishment, suggested that she should take advantage of staying there with Gordon by going through the basic treatment herself. This she did – somewhat unwillingly, since she always liked to say that there was nothing wrong with her. However when she came home she found that several of her own minor health problems had also disappeared.

Later in the same year, Brian, who was in his third year at Trinity College Dublin, realised that he was recognising a vocation for himself to the ministry of the Church of Ireland. Gordon was understandably thrilled by this news. He already had the joy of seeing both Peter and Ruth commit themselves fully to working under the disciplines of the principles of MRA. These ideas had proved a totally fulfilling element in his own work, both when on a full-time basis with the MRA teams, and also in his work with the

Church. Now one of his sons was planning to follow his footsteps into the ministry.

Compared with Gordon's own absolute certainty from his earliest years that his future lay in the ministry, Brian readily admits that in his case it was a much more gradual process. His growing awareness of a calling was constantly encouraged by seeing the Church and the Parish in Rostrevor coming back to life under inspired leadership. He writes, "I loved what I saw and experienced as a member of the parish family, including the traditional but lively services, the choir-singing, the bell-ringing, the life-changing stories and listening to my father preach."

His sense of vocation also grew through a great friendship with a fellow student who already knew that his own future was to be in the Church. He remembers being much inspired by listening to talks and taking part in discussions with various visitors to TCD such as Michael Ramsay, who at the time was Archbishop of York and who had come to lead a mission at the College. Another who challenged him greatly was Bishop Wilson of Birmingham who preached in the College Chapel. He had spent time in a Japanese prisoner-of-war camp and had gone back after the war to confirm one of his Japanese warders.

In the course of putting this book together, there has been a constant supply of reminiscence and encouragement from my sister Ruth and my four brothers. Many of these have already been quoted. When Michael, the youngest of the family, sent his personal memories he gave them the heading 'On Coming Last'. As he was born six years after Brian, there were many times when he felt very much on his own. When he sent a copy of his thoughts to Leslie, by now an American citizen, he triggered some similar ideas in his oldest brother's mind. Hilda had lost a still-born child in 1926 which meant that there was a four-year gap between Leslie and Peter. As a result, Leslie also grew up with a certain sense of loneliness at the other end of the family.

The whole question of Gordon's relationships with the family has been touched on earlier, but at this stage, it comes up again following the impact of Brian's decision about his future. Although Brian never formally became a member of 'the MRA team', he willingly recognises the tremendous 'added value' he gained from the environment of his youth which he was able to use consistently throughout his own ministry.

He particularly identifies:- '(1) The strength of Christian morality. (2) The sense of guidance from, and absolute commitment to, the God who loves you and speaks to you. (3) Openness to and friendship with every other human being who is equally loved by God. (4) Being part of a mission to God's world that supersedes all of our internal denominational divisions.' He sums it up. 'The Church of Ireland, with Dad's support, was the appropriate environment for me to exercise that mission.'

It is interesting to note that both Michael and Leslie felt themselves under considerable pressure to become involved with MRA. Leslie took the opportunity of his years in the RAF to think through his own future and made his own decision. Michael writes of feeling similar strong influences and pressures during his adolescent and teenage years and continues, " The 'swinging sixties' had just begun when I went up to Trinity and I was determined to make the most of my new freedom from school and what I felt was an increasingly cramped home life – I was the only 'child' left at home."

Although three of the family followed careers which were to make them independent from MRA (which remained Gordon's guiding principle to the end of his life), something which all of his children learnt over the years can be summed up in a remark made to Frank Buchman by Sir Richard Livingstone, a one-time Vice-Chancellor of Oxford University. Garth Lean quotes the remark in 'Frank Buchman - a Life'.

Sir Richard said, *"When you and I were young, there were moral fences. We did not always keep to them, but we always knew when we crossed them."*

Although the six of us were all from a different generation, it is fair to say that Gordon and Hilda taught us about 'moral fences'. We knew what and where they were, and, speaking for myself, I always knew when I had crossed them. I still do!

By 1958, Leslie had been working for several years for a company called Production Engineering which specialised in developing good management practice in industry. The work took the form of consultancy attachments to a wide variety of companies in different parts of the world.

After leaving South Africa, Leslie had worked briefly in Nigeria and then he and Pat moved on to Australia where their oldest son Philip was born in Sidney. Now in 1958, his latest job was in Dublin. By a happy coincidence, while Leslie and Pat were in Dublin, Peter made his first visit home from Africa, and the whole family were together for the first time since 1950. The photograph taken at the time shows Gordon and Hilda with their six children, together with Leslie's wife Pat, holding their first grandchild, and all joined by the ever faithful Florrie Dowds.

Gordon's health had recovered sufficiently for him to be able to carry on with his parochial responsibilities and to keep on with his work with the Churches' Industrial Council which continued to meet regularly. By this stage, Bill Boyd had joined the group, and he remembers that they found themselves concentrating to a great extent on social issues and the Churches' responsibilities in those fields. There were no particular efforts to take an overtly evangelising stance; they were, rather, more concerned to show that the Churches cared about all those involved in the industrial scene in its widest sense and that men led by God could contribute positively to the hard life of the real world. They also witnessed by their togetherness to the fact that the unifying factors of Christianity could cross what far too many people in Ulster believed to be impenetrable barriers.

Meanwhile in the parish the programme of restoration and re-furbishment of the Church continued and a great number of gifts for use in the building were accepted and consecrated by Bishop Mitchell at a special Thanksgiving Service. The evening before the service, the Bishop had stayed at the Vicarage and demonstrated his skills at the piano, taking off his frock coat, which he always wore, and sitting in all the glory of shirt-sleeves and braces while he hammered out songs from Gilbert and Sullivan's operas. He was well supported by Hilda, Ruth and myself who at the time were the mainstays of the church choir.

This picture of all the family was taken on the day of the Baptism of Gordon's first grandchild Philip.

Back row L-R :- Michael, Brian, Ruth, Florrie(Philip's Godmother), David and Peter.
Front row L-R :- Hilda. Gordon, Pat with Philip on her knee and Leslie.

Gordon and Hilda's six children were not to meet together again for 40 years. See Appendix C

Shortly after this visit, the Bishop gave me a personal licence to act as a Diocesan Lay Reader under Gordon's direction and at his discretion. This was principally to allow me to help lighten the physical burden which continued to bear fairly heavily on Gordon's shoulders.

I wrote three short sermons never lasting more than five minutes and all based within the limitations of my own experience, practice and belief. When Gordon asked me to take Evening Service for him on Trinity Sunday I sat down to write my five minutes on my concept of the Trinity. As always, I showed it to Gordon. He read it carefully and handed it back with the words, "I understand exactly what you're trying to say. It's very clear. There's just one slight problem: it's all heresy!"

Any time I have told that story to other clergy, they have laughed and have usually said something like "Why do you think that rectors who are lucky enough to have curates always make sure they are down to preach on that Festival Sunday?"

* * * * * * *

By the end of 1959 it was becoming increasingly obvious that even though Gordon's health had improved, it would not stand up much longer to the continuing strain of running the parish and he advised the Bishop of his wish to retire.

The principal aims of his ministry in Rostrevor had been achieved. Kilbroney Parish was very much a lively and going concern. There was by now a trained core of lay people who had learnt how to play their part in ensuring that that liveliness would continue. The church building was sound, extensively repaired and renovated. The Vicarage was in excellent order and would be ready to welcome the next incumbent with open arms.

The date was set for his retirement, and on Sunday 29th May 1960, the Sunday after Ascension Day, Gordon preached his farewell sermon.

Retirement

The first problem facing Gordon and Hilda when retirement loomed was to find somewhere to live. Many years before, when Hilda's younger brother Jim died, tragically while still a young man, he had left her a legacy of £2,000 in his will. Hilda had used the money to buy a holiday house in Portballintrae on the North Antrim coast. After the war, in 1946, that house was sold and another was bought in Ballycastle. It was used for family holidays in August and was rented out at other times.

Mention has been made earlier of James Faulkner (*see p.102*) who had remained a good friend over the years. When he realised that Gordon and Hilda were looking for somewhere to live, he offered them the opportunity to buy an enormous house next door to his own at a price that bore very little relationship to its true market value. By selling the Ballycastle house, Gordon and Hilda were able to take advantage of this very generous gesture and moved into their new home. Recalling echoes of his earliest days, Gordon decided to call the house Ardreigh, the same name as the old family home in Athy.

Shortly after the family moved into Ardreigh, my wife Joan Conn and I were married in July 1960. Gordon was invited to take part in the service by the minister of Joan's church. Again the notes of what he said survive. Among them, these words:

"God is Love. That is the heart of this service. The Cross is the language God chose that everyman could understand – the symbol of Love is the supreme giving of God that we might have Life. *Love* and *Life*. Today each of you said to the other 'I will' – a vow for life. A promise becomes a vow when it is made to God. Saying 'I will' to God for your whole life is the best guarantee of it to each other. Today you face the adventure of a new home – not only a place of happiness for yourselves, but a base from which He can operate to bring order and beauty out of chaos, and heal the wounds of a distracted world. This will not happen by chance. This marriage was made in heaven – let it be directed by heaven.

"Anyone who thinks he can get more out of life than God can is a fool! It takes God to build a home. This is something of what is meant when we say Love is the key to Life. Have responsibility for each other as God wants you to be."

Brian was my best man, but it was only later that I learnt that the day had brought him a great shock. He tells the story in his own words.

"It was in that first year of Dad's retirement that I had my first really heart-searching experience of life, with a direct parallel in his own. I had been happily engaged for some time, but when ordination was my future and my fiancée was dedicated to nursing in London, it became clear that this marriage was not 'made in heaven' and she had the courage to say so. For one of the very few times in my life, my Dad sat down with me at my invitation, and we talked it all through and he shared his similar experience with me. I told him how hard I was finding it to let go, and after we had had some time of quiet reflection, he said to me, 'Brian, do you love her enough to set her free, so that she may one day marry the right person for her?' That made good Christian loving sense to me, and when a few years later I too found 'the right person', who was as surprised as I was by 'God's choice' for us both, we lived and loved and grew and shared responsibilities beyond our wildest dreams."

When James Faulkner sold the house, he showed Hilda plans which he had made to convert the building into apartments. At this stage their financial situation was based only on Gordon's State and Church of Ireland pensions, since Hilda had not yet reached pensionable age. As a result, when she looked at the plans for the building, Hilda realised that it would be possible to convert parts of it into flats and still keep plenty of room for the family. This would give them an additional source of income.

The first project was to convert the ballroom (an area of 1000 square feet) plus a small existing bathroom in the main house into a two bedroom flat. At later stages two further areas were also converted; one was made from the second floor of the main house and the other from what had been a laundry and other utility areas under the ballroom flat.

Although Gordon had retired from his parish work, he continued to keep in touch with his friends and colleagues from the Churches' Industrial Council, maintaining friendships which lasted for many years. He also felt it right to make Ardreigh available as a meeting place for the other people in Northern Ireland who were still working through their lives on the continuing basis of MRA.

In 1963 he was invited to attend the Christus Rex Congress in Tullamore together with his friend Bill Boyd from the Industrial Council. As Gordon was no longer fit to drive, Hilda took him to Portadown where they met up with Bill, and the two men travelled on in his car. When they arrived at the Congress they were delighted to be greeted by Cahal Daly who was acting as Guest Master. When he introduced Gordon to the meeting, he used his old title of Archdeacon Hannon – a courtesy which many people used, even though it was more than twenty years since he had held the office.

Bill Boyd remembers, with amusement, many of those present being very impressed by this dignitary coming among them and the conviction many of them had that he himself must be Gordon's personal chaplain – an interesting combination of Anglican and Presbyterian ministries!

The principal guest speaker at the Congress was Shirley Williams whose main theme was the Pursuit of Social Justice. She was a committed Roman Catholic, and at the time was very much a rising star in the British Labour Party. Although Gordon and Bill were the only Protestants among the company, Gordon was in his element and, as Bill puts it, "When he spoke, he really made people sit up and take notice. He still had a fire about him and a powerful personality."

There can be little doubt that in those days in the early 1960's, Gordon still had that fire. Some excerpts from a sermon preached in St. Anne's Cathedral in Belfast give a taste of the message. Gordon's favourite modern translation of the New Testament was by Phillips, and his chosen text was from Romans 8 verses 19 & 20. *"The whole creation is on tip-toe to see the wonderful sight of the sons of God coming into their own . . . . . the magnificent liberty which can only belong to the Children of God."*

"If the Apostle Paul were in this pulpit today, he would proclaim the same answer that he wrote to his friends in Rome – the great metropolis of his world, the heart of an empire that had no place for the Christian God, or at any rate meant to keep that God in his place.

"If you take the trouble to read the whole of this wonderful letter, you will notice three things.

> 1. He has no blinkers on about the world he is dealing with – the setting in which the Great Idea has to operate.
> 2. Nothing can dim or damp his faith.
> 3. If the nation and the world is to get the Idea, it must come through ordinary people, no matter what their job, whose one purpose in life is to live it and give it.

Think about the world we live in. In spite of all God has done for us through countless ages,

> We refuse to honour Him as God
> We put Man in God's place
> We worship the Creature instead of the Creator

And so God has given us up to the vileness of our own devisings. Paul would have no blinkers on about us and our disappearing moral standards."

Gordon describes how Communism still mocks 'so-called Christians.'

"Communism only succeeds when we refuse to live our Christianity. We leave all those other people under their control, with their problems unanswered, as we fall easy victims to a philosophy that puts profits, wages, property, power - before people and elevates Man to take the place of God.

"It is a solemn experience for a Priest of God, one commissioned to give God's Answer, to look back over half a century of life in this island of Ireland.

> Two World Wars
> A bloody revolution
> An even more bloody Civil War
> The Blaming. The Pointing of the Finger.

The Fears and Suspicions.
The Compromise.
The constant rush to the Press to stymie any effort to get together
The passion with which we argue about *Who* is right
The reluctance to unite for *What* is right
The huddling in our own self-centred spiritual corners.

"Well, it was in just such a world that Paul issued his challenge to Christians to take up the task as the Sons of God. Today the torch is handed to us. I have always had a vision of what this Cathedral could be in the City and in the Nation.

"Suppose each one of us was to make now a clear-cut decision to go out and to be the answer to our prayers, to fight for the things we profess to believe in. No need for any of us to remain stuffy, pious or pompous – smug, self-centred or self-satisfied – nor, again, defensive, divisive, defeated or, above all, deadly dull.

"God's New World can walk out of this Church on your legs and on mine!

"I remember the day God told me that He couldn't give a living faith to those around me, as long as I continued in His place. God is looking for a complete right of way through us into our common life. Think of it – a completely new impetus; a new purpose and motive. To let God be God. To quit for ever accepting standards lower than we know are right in our *private* and *business* lives and in *public affairs*. Listening and obeying without compromise.

"No problem need remain unsolved if God is given the green light through us. In one week men could be talking about revolution, revival, renaissance. And Ireland can become the Reconciler of Nations.

"The world simply aches for a picture of what Christianity is meant to be!"

Gordon's surviving sermon notes show that he was still being invited to preach until he was well into his 80's. With fire like that, it should come as no surprise.

Changes

On the domestic front, Gordon's life in retirement was greatly influenced by family events such as weddings, education plans, career changes and, above all, by decisions about where he and Hilda would make their final home.

In 1961, before Hilda's work on converting parts of Ardreigh into flats began to come to fruition and to provide additional sources of income, they were struggling to live on Gordon's state pension combined with the tiny pension to which he was entitled under the Church of Ireland scheme in operation at that time. Although he had been in the ordained ministry for some forty-four years, Gordon had not been serving in any official or salaried capacity for the fourteen years between 1940 and 1954.

Ever since 1936, when she first came to work in Lurgan Rectory, Florrie Dowds had been an integral part of the family. Originally employed as a nurse/nanny to look after Brian, in 1940 she made the decision to come to Wolfhill on much the same basis as Gordon's own decision. Over the years since then, Gordon and Hilda had felt it right to give her a small annual allowance that would give her some degree of financial independence.

Now, unfortunately, when they moved into Ardreigh, the costs of keeping the house going meant that money was very tight. After much soul searching, it was decided that Florrie should look for a post that would bring in a reliable salary. Shortly after the decision was taken, she found a place as companion to an elderly lady of somewhat uncertain temperament who lived in Holywood. This was near enough various members of the family for Florrie to be able to keep in regular contact. That first job was comparatively short-lived and she moved on to take a bigger responsibility looking after a residential home for trainee nurses.

In 1962 Hilda's mother died at the age of 93. Known to one and all as 'Granny Denny' she and Hilda's father, Leslie Denny (who died in 1936) had accepted the challenge of the ideas of the Oxford Group as an enrichment of their Christian lives. Gordon preached at her funeral. In part he said:-

"I remember after Leslie Denny died, and their son Jim, Granny Denny wrote me a wonderful letter which I shall always treasure. It has helped many people. In it she said – 'Of course I miss them terribly, but I feel them with me all the time, and sorrow is transcended into joy.' Those are the notes for our hearts today – Life and Joy, and Gratitude to God for so many things. For all her 93 years. For so many memories. What a gift she was with all her happy vital personality.

"I think specially of her caring for people. For all of us in her own family, increasing as the years went by. I met Mrs Denny first between the wars. Typical of her then was all she put into the Memorial Hall at Castlecatt. There had been such colossal loss of splendid lives and of so much that was precious in Europe.

"Then there came a growing consciousness that we had not the answer for Germany, nor indeed for ourselves. Things seemed to be drifting towards something even worse. There was a lack of something big enough to live for, to give everything for together. These islands were in no sense 'A world fit for heroes.' At that time the conviction began to form in some of us that Britain still had a destiny among the nations; that she could give the lead that was so badly needed, if we would rise to it. The truth began to dawn that there was little use waiting for other people or pointing the finger at other people. The answer must begin within ourselves. We must cease running our own show. We must let God be God. The simple truths of the Bible must begin to live again. In every age, absolute moral standards accepted by His people had been the key to God's plan for the nation and the world. With that came a new sense of sin and a new sense of the miracle of God's grace. Very simply it meant less of self and more of God. This meant for many of us a new beginning, a new orientation of life, a new relevance of all that the Church stood for and the constant vision that Britain must be governed (in every department of her life) by men who are governed by God.

"Mr. and Mrs. Denny's reactions were interesting. Their background was Conservative, the relics of a feudal society. They were good; they did good work, they had a fine sense of responsibility. Such people often dislike change, they don't like their set ways being disturbed. But with them, on the contrary, their response was immediate and whole-hearted. Granny Denny never lost this over-ruling passion for a new world built on new people, through the change of human nature, beginning in oneself. The old truth took on a new meaning – man was planned to be a new creation in Christ Jesus. Like all of us, she had many things to learn because she loved her own way and her own plans. In fact she had the faults of her virtues.

"These last months have been very tough for her. Some people seem to have been chosen to be cross-bearers, to share the sufferings of our Lord. One day when things were really bad, I said to her, 'You've been a good fighter and are not going to give up the fight at this stage.' We talked of what Jesus said, 'In the world ye shall have tribulation; but courage, I have overcome the world.' She looked up with her old twinkle and said, 'Guts!'

"Mrs Denny had so many gifts and privileges, capable, forceful, able, and she didn't suffer fools gladly. No Government Department, County or Rural Council awed her. She fought fearlessly for what she believed to be right. Such people can easily become self-sufficient, even dictatorial. That happens when life is centred on self rather than in God. In these last days some of the old hymns were most helpful to her:

'I need Thy presence every passing hour;
What but Thy grace can foil the tempter's power?
Who like Thyself my guide and stay can be?
Help of the helpless, O abide with me.'

"I cannot close without mention of the love she inspired in those around her. All her large family circle down to her great-grandchildren longed to express our gratitude and caring. But I'm thinking specially of those who tended her through these last months of illness. For them nothing was a burden. So now, as we commit her into God's hands, our best memorial to her, certainly what would be dearest to her heart, is to commit ourselves afresh to God and to one another, daily to live under His orders, united together in Him, instruments in His hands, and through His grace sharing in the working out of His perfect plan."

* * * * *

Granny Denny in her garden at the Basket House, Castlecatt, Co. Antrim.

Arriving with Eva McBain at David and Joan's wedding

By this time, all the younger generation had left home except for Michael, who was still at Trinity,. Leslie and his family had moved permanently to America; Peter was in Africa; Joan and I were beginning to raise our own family in Holywood as I worked in television with the BBC; Ruth was beginning her four-year stint as a lecturer at Stranmillis Teacher Training College; Brian was a Curate in All Saints Parish, Clooney in Londonderry.

Gordon and Hilda both had a great love for the North Antrim area and they bought a large second-hand caravan which they were able to set up semi-permanently on a small site by the sea near Ballycastle. With Gordon's health always a problem, they tried to get away to the caravan fairly often so that they could get a complete rest from stress and strain.

The next major change in the situation arose when Peter came home from Africa in 1964. He had spent a long time in Nigeria which is a country where most people from overseas working there are encouraged to take a major break of at least three months every two years. Apart from some shorter visits to Caux in Switzerland accompanying friends and contacts from West Africa, Peter had not taken a proper break since 1958. The cumulative effects of this long period in tropical conditions had obviously caught up with him and he was clearly not at all well.

He was eventually diagnosed as suffering from Ménière's disease and it was possible to begin treatment which had to be combined with complete rest. At one stage he and Gordon went up to Ballycastle to stay in the caravan and he had the opportunity of re-establishing contact between them as they both caught up with events since his last visit home.

Meanwhile, up in Londonderry, Brian had met Maeve Butler – the experience which he mentioned in his story quoted earlier in the 'Rostrevor' chapter. As a serving Curate in the Church of Ireland in those days, he was not allowed to marry. However things changed the moment he was appointed to his first parish as Rector of Desertmartin. The Institution took place in September 1964 and just two days later they were married and took off on their honeymoon. With Peter home, all the family except Leslie were there for the occasion.

In 1965, the play 'Mr. Wilberforce' was brought to Belfast. The play centred around the life of William Wilberforce, the great abolitionist, and was the latest in a series written by Alan Thornhill, the author of 'The Forgotten Factor'.

The Westminster Theatre in London had been bought as a memorial to the MRA team members who had lost their lives in the War. It regularly staged most of the plays which had been written by men such as Alan Thornhill and Peter Howard to take the message of people accepting God's control in their lives to many parts of the world.

As usually happened when the plays went 'on tour', the cast was accompanied by a team of people who would be in place to follow up questions and challenges raised in the minds of the audiences. On this occasion the team included Fiona Graham who was staying with an old school friend, Heather Boyd. Heather turned out to be a highly successful matchmaker who made it her business to throw Peter and Fiona into each other's paths.

That her plans had succeeded was demonstrated when Peter's proposal of marriage was accepted on April 16th 1966. That particular date in the calendar has a strange resonance in the family as it was the birthday of both Gordon and Ruth – as well as Hilda's brother Edward!

Peter and Fiona were married in October that year and they then stayed in London for several months, supporting a long-time Nigerian friend in dubbing the all-African film 'Freedom' into Hausa. In 1968 they moved back to Belfast and took over the Ballroom Flat in Ardreigh. At the time, the main part of the house had been let as well as the other flats. Gordon and Hilda had begun to live permanently in the caravan in Ballycastle.

Later in 1968 the sad news came through that Florrie Dowds had died. She had never been a particularly strong person physically, although her personal strength had always been plain to see. After a period of poor health, she was diagnosed with cancer some eighteen months earlier and, once the disease took control of her life, she had spent her last months being cared for by her own family.

Gordon wrote the following piece for publication in local Lurgan papers.

In Memoriam: Florence Mabel Dowds

Very quietly and without fuss, a gracious woman, of whom Lurgan may well be proud, passed from us some weeks ago – Florrie Dowds.

I knew her from childhood and later she came to live with us in the old Shankill Rectory. Our family owe her a deep debt for her loving care inspired by a living faith which expressed itself in responsibility for community, country and the world of the future. This outward look meant much to our family who were her special care.

When war came, she had been with us for some years and she decided, with us, to renounce security and in 1940 to give ourselves to our war effort in applying our Christian experience to the special problems of relationships in industry and in government. Florrie was invaluable in this work so vital to our community life and which today, so many years later is still as much the concern of all the Churches.

After the war, Florrie's great sense of responsibility freed my wife and me for spells of using our special training and experience in some world trouble spots.

Later, when I was Rector of Rostrevor, Florrie was a much loved Sunday School Superintendent. When I retired from active parochial life, she took on a responsible job in Belfast caring for candidate nurses.

Her long and painful illness was faced in a courageous and faith-filled way that did wonders for many people in and outside of her immediate family.

To us, as part of the inner group who knew and loved her deeply and saw her great qualities spread in widening circles, we acclaim her as a worthy citizen of Lurgan and hope to follow in her train.

* * * * *

Florrie at Rathmore

Although Gordon and Hilda now lived permanently in their caravan, Hilda launched herself on a series of building projects involving conversions, restorations and the re-structuring of various abandoned or redundant properties.

The first of these was an old School Hall belonging to Ramoan Parish on the outskirts of Ballycastle. With the help of government grants, the building was converted into a two-storey structure with a small extension. While the work was in hand, under her direct supervision as her own Clerk of Works, Hilda developed the garden – so that house and garden were up and running by the time they moved in. Under the terms of the grants legislation, they had to live in the house for at least two years before they could sell it.

At this time Peter and Fiona had decided to stay in Northern Ireland for some time and continue working there. When Granny Denny died in 1962, Hilda had become a beneficiary under her father's Will which meant that she had a life interest in the third of his estate which he had ultimately bequeathed to his Hannon grandchildren. In a series of generous gestures, Hilda convinced the Trustees of the Will that some capital sums should be released to the members of the family at times of particular need.

Gordon and Hilda knew from their own experience what Peter and Fiona were facing as people who had made the decision to dedicate their lives to working on a full-time basis with MRA, where there was no salary and no financial security. After consultations with the rest of the family and with their support, rather than releasing another capital sum through the Trustees, they made the decision to give Ardreigh to Peter and Fiona. This would provide them at least with a base for the future.

It is often said that moving house comes second only to marriage in its ability to create stress, but for Gordon and Hilda it was to become a way of life for the next ten years. As soon as they were settled into a house, they would drive round the countryside looking for another suitable property. Hilda had a great eye for recognising potential. Not many would have spotted the old schoolmaster's house and school near Moss-side. It had been half demolished to improve sight-lines at a crossroads. Hilda worked out that it could be restored by cleaning up and buttressing the half-wrecked end, and then building an extension at the other. She soon became a master at the art of convincing the planning authorities of the validity of her proposals, after which she would set about supervising construction and, as always, designing and making the new garden.

Each of the first four of these properties was bought for next to nothing and the restoration and modification work was carried out at minimal cost by direct labour; only the plumbing and electrical work had to be carried out by qualified experts. Hilda could often be seen driving about the country with her trailer loaded with breeze-blocks, sacks of cement, bags of plaster or Bangor Blue slates. As a result, when the houses were eventually sold, they each showed a considerable profit. This made a difference to their finances and made it possible for them to maintain a reasonable standard of living.

In April 1971, Peter and Fiona threw a great party in Ardreigh to celebrate Gordon's 80th birthday. The day turned into a double celebration when, to everyone's delight, Ruth announced her engagement to David Howden Hume, a Scot who shared her ideals. They had met while she was still teaching in London and had come over together for the party.

The entertainment at the party included a sketch featuring Brian in frock coat playing the part of a young and rather pompous 'Archdeacon', while Ruth (caricaturing Hilda) also appeared, brandishing a hockey stick and wearing an Ulster Inter-provincial Red Hand on her shirt. Sadly, no copy of the script exists.

In October of that same year, Ruth and David were married in Ballycastle. They lived in London until they returned to Northern Ireland with their daughter Frances in 1977.

After completing his studies at Trinity, Michael had made two forays into the world of business, first as a management trainee and then in sales.

Gordon and Hilda enjoying the fun at his 80th birthday party.

Ruth nd Brian providing the etertainment,

Neither brought him the prospect of career satisfaction, but serendipity saw to it that he became involved in the world of libraries. During his training at Queen's University, he met Rosemary Howard and they in turn were married on New Year's Day 1972.

The next big family event occurred on 11th April 1973 and took place in Gordon and Hilda's third home, a converted blacksmith's forge with two attached cottages near Armoy. By then, Joan and I had returned from my two years with the Malawi Broadcasting Corporation and were back with the BBC in Leicester. Michael describes the day: "The highlight of that year was the Golden Wedding Celebration at Billy Parish Church for which I played the organ and Rosemary baked the cake. It was a wonderfully happy occasion for which Pop wrote one of his better poems!"

This was a reference to a family tradition which Gordon had begun many years earlier. Almost any significant event in the family would lead to Gordon producing some poetic tribute. Some of them were inclined to be doggerel – although the sentiments expressed were genuine enough. For this special occasion he produced the following:

Golden Wedding Day – Wednesday 11th April 1973

Ten, 20, 30, 40, 50 years! But first what went before –
True gold appeared not far off County Antrim shore.
On Balcony of Whins* the moon shone full and clear   *(* Hilda's Home)*
On gold that left me speechless, oh so very dear.
Boxing Day Meet – we and the horses jumped stone walls with joy
The dance at Trocadero confirmed the true alloy.
Father Denny, when asked, said Yes – sound advice, most encouraging of people;
Mother Denny, beaming, warned – She'll climb the Church's steeple"!
The good news spreads; Ballymoney open wide their eyes
My Rectory sister registers her glad surprise.
Old history this, but, friends, not half the facts are told
For each day new wonders. Gold, yes real Gold.

Gordon and Hilda returning to Billy Parish Church - Grandson Tony in the lead.

Golden Wedding Celebrations

Brian leading the service: Michael at the organ.

Saidie Patterson greeting Hilda and Gordon at the celebration.

Gordon Hannon

Then fifty years with wife and mother till this Golden Wedding Day
When loved ones gather round us in lovely bright array.
Great years – one lovely daughter, five fine healthy sons
One extra son, world statesman, five extra daughters and each one's
More beautiful, more precious and if possible more dear!
Nor yet indeed have we the picture wholly, fully clear –
Grandchildren! First-borns Philip, Patrick, Desmond, Catherine –
I count eleven
For Gran and Poppa, one word will do – that's heaven.

Pride! Yes Pride! Indeed we had, yes that is really true,
While Ireland, poor tragic Ireland, what is she to do? –
God's finger points at me, perhaps at you, "You badly need more grace;
You Irish talk and talk, while each one tries to take My place.
Remember this. As you are so is the nation –
North, South, East and West whatever is your station.
No twisting, no wavering, just simply this – *the true White Paper Poll*
Give o'er to God, yes you, *His rightful full control.*"

More Gold each day – Yes fresh Gold each and every day
While daily to God we listen and try promptly to obey.
New men and women, and yes, new boys and girls
While wider, still world wider His loving circle whirls.

So – *A New World* for each, for all
This Golden Wedding Day
As I step down, God's love shines forth
With His true Golden Ray.

Hilda **Hannon** **Gordon**

Time moved on. Hilda still worked on houses. At the other end of Armoy village she found another old forge beside the banks of the River Bush. This time it was more a matter of restoration. Unfortunately, Gordon was beginning to lose the strength in his legs and he found the steepness of the paths around the house and down towards the river becoming more and more difficult to deal with.

Then, without warning, in 1975, Hilda was taken ill and had to go into hospital. By this time Peter and Fiona had decided to go back to work in South Africa and all the rest of the family were living in England. It was decided that Gordon should fly to London and spend a while with Ruth and David before moving on to visit Michael and Rosemary.

Michael describes what happened during the visit:-

"Pop wasn't at all well while staying with us. He had a high fever and severe gastric problems which required constant nursing and bed-bathing by Rosemary and myself. That week of very personal physical care was something of a turning point in my relationship with him: a new friendship, warmth and affection blossomed between us."

Elsewhere in his notes, Michael makes other comments on his relationship with Gordon:-

"I have always regretted not having known him in his prime as a young 'Dad', a regret which I think, he shared too. Our difference in age, almost a two-generational gap, must have had something to do with it. Sometimes he would surprise me with a small and loving gesture. One of my most prized possessions is a set of Sheffield-made chisels which, quite out of the blue, Pop brought home for me one day from a tool shop in Newry – an inspired idea, as it turned out. It meant that I could really develop my woodworking skills, which I still practise today, using those same chisels.

"I was sorry not to have seen more of Pop in his later declining years. He and I had had our differences. I had never felt the 'call' and had shied away from MRA. I think that we both regretted that we had never really known each other in an open, uncomplicated father-and-son sort of way, but later in life he and I had got to know each other much better and were much closer than we'd ever been in earlier times. I'm happy to remember him now with great respect, warmth and affection and gratitude for the values he stood for and passed down the line."

Hilda made one further attempt to sort out another house – this time a bungalow on the edge of Moss-side which Hilda described as 'a very Protestant neighbourhood' . Throughout all the times of working on the houses she had recruited a team who were used to working together. Most of them were from Ballycastle, a place with a mainly Roman Catholic population. Hilda always made her decisions about things on the basis of getting the best man for the job. As it turned out, most of her building team were Catholics. Hilda describes what happened:-

"On the basis of giving me a friendly warning, one of the inhabitants told me that if I went on employing nothing but Catholics I might get shot! I told him that I never enquired what a man's religion was, and that I would go on employing whoever I wanted. Sure enough, about a fortnight later, we did get a shot through one of the windows – such a neat, inoffensive round hole – as long as you weren't in the line of fire! We took no notice except to make special friends with some of our fiery Protestant neighbours. A few days later we woke up to find a fresh salmon outside the front door! One of the neighbours told me I needn't have a bit of worry, 'Sure the lads round here would murder anyone who touched you!'

"By the time I had restored that little house, it became obvious that I must spend all my time with Gordon as he began to take weak turns and sometimes even fell down – though he never hurt himself. He couldn't get up by himself and I found it very hard to lift him. As I struggled to help, there were times when we both collapsed on the floor in fits of giggles!

"Gordon used to love his walks with me pushing him in his wheelchair, the fresh air was so good for him. However, the family felt strongly that we should try to move back into Ballycastle. We agreed.

"Just then a very strange and rather moving thing happened. Dr. Stewart – who at the time was not our doctor - was talking to me about some work he was doing on a bungalow he was building for his retirement in the orchard behind his own house. He suddenly said, 'You wouldn't like to buy my house, would you?' This was exactly the sort of opportunity we had been discussing with the family.

"I brought Gordon to see the house and he loved it, saying it reminded him of his old family home."

The house was suitable in many ways since it could be converted into flats and Hilda and Gordon would be able to live on the ground floor. However they were not to enjoy it together for long.

After a few happy months in this final home, Gordon's health took its last turn for the worse and Hilda was no longer able to cope with the physical difficulties of the full-time caring which he needed. In October 1977 he was moved into the Dalriada Hospital in Ballycastle. This is a small Cottage Hospital where Gordon was given a private room. While he received regular nursing care from the staff, Hilda was encouraged to visit him as often as she wished, and she made a habit of helping with his feeding, as he was too weak to manage it on his own.

Ruth remembers visiting him, with her daughter Frances, when they went to see him towards the end.

"It must have been hard for him not to have the mental and physical energies he used to. As he lay in bed, I said to him, 'Well I've got a good man now!' Dad struggled and managed to say with a smile, 'As long as he be- behaves himself!' and with a twinkle in his eye he called a quiet 'Toodle-oodle-oo!' to Frances."

Hilda wrote:- "Near the end he couldn't speak, but he could understand everything and one of the things he specially loved was to listen to David on tape, reading favourite parts of the Bible.

"About a week before he died, Brian and Maeve came to see him. They brought their three boys aged 12, 10 and 8 and I asked Brian if it was right that they should see their beloved grandfather in such a state. Brian thought for a few moments and then said, 'These boys have known nothing but violent death all around them in Derry and I think they should have the chance of seeing what truly peaceful Christian dying can be like.' I agreed and they all kissed 'Poppa' who knew them and smiled at each one – Desmond, Brendan and Neil."

A few days later, Brian was with Hilda as Gordon lay dying. As he looks back, he too remembers:

"I was so glad to be able to minister to him in simple Church of Ireland style, to feel close to him and my mother as we sat and talked and prayed with him, committing him quietly to the One for whom he had ultimate love, and Who he knew had ultimate love for him, for us and for every human being. I read to him my favourite hymn which I knew united us in that love. Here it is.

> 'It were my soul's desire
> to see the face of God;
> It were my soul's desire
> to rest in His abode.
> It were my soul's desire
> a spirit free from gloom,
> It were my soul's desire
> new life beyond the doom.
>
> It were my soul's desire
> to study zealously;
> this, too, my soul's desire
> a clear rule set for me.
> Grant, Lord, my soul's desire,
> deep waves of cleansing sighs,
> grant, Lord, my soul's desire,
> from earthly cares to rise.
>
> It were my soul's desire
> to shun the doom of hell;
> yet more my soul's desire
> within His house to dwell.
> It were my soul's desire
> to imitate my King;
> it were my soul's desire
> His endless praise to sing.

It were my soul's desire
when heaven's gate is won,
to find my soul's desire
clear shining like the sun.
This still my soul's desire
whatever life afford,
to gain my soul's desire
and see Thy face, O Lord.

"Peacefully, Gordon Hannon died. Hilda gently closed his eyes. We kissed him and left him in God's hands."

Michael remembers the funeral:

"It was a wonderfully joyous and moving occasion and I was very proud to have been one of his coffin-bearers. But one particular incident remains with me which seems to capture something of the spirit of Pop and Mama's later years in and around North Antrim. About half an hour before the service, I walked into Ramoan Parish Church where Pop's coffin was resting on trestles. Mary Dallatt, an old Roman Catholic friend was embracing the coffin and apparently talking to Pop in confidential whispers. She heard me approaching and said: 'He was a wonderful man, the Archdeacon, and I'm just here saying a wee bye-bye to him.'"

Hilda's memories begin with almost the identical words:

"Gordon's funeral was a truly triumphant occasion and really worthy of him. The church was filled to overflowing, and every sort and condition of people who came showed the love and veneration in which he was held. From down and outs to Members of Parliament, clergy of all denominations, including priests and nuns who had been visiting him in hospital. From England, Scotland and all over Ireland they came. My workmen were there and such a help to us all. Alan Thornhill, Gordon's old friend and companion on visits to America, gave a very fine address*, while our son David read the lesson beautifully. The Archdeacon of Connor, the Ven. William McCappin, read the prayers and Bishop Arthur Butler said the prayers of committal at the graveside. Both were old friends.

* For full text of Rev. Alan Thornhill's address see Appendix B

"We sang Gordon's favourite hymns – 'The Lord's my Shepherd', then 'Dear Lord and Father of mankind' and finally, with a tremendous shout of triumph, 'Praise, my soul, the King of Heaven'. The singing was out of this world. His three youngest sons, together with his one and only son-in-law, carried his coffin to the graveside.

"When we were having tea at the house afterwards, Joan, David's wife, said to me, 'You know, Granny, it's almost like a party. I expect to see Poppa coming into the room at any minute.' - and indeed it was; his loving spirit was all around us."

Gordon Hannon

Appendix A

In 1937, Frank Buchman issued a manifesto under the title 'The Destiny of Nations'. It read:

'By a miracle of science, men can speak by radio to millions. By a miracle of the Spirit, God can speak to every man. His voice can be heard in every home, every business, every government.
When man listens, God speaks.
When man obeys, God acts.

It does not matter who you are or where you are. Accurate, adequate information can come from the Mind of God to the minds of men who are willing to take their orders from Him.

This is the revolution which will end revolutions by changing human nature and remaking men and nations.

People believe that their leaders should be guided by God. But the rank and file must be guided too. A God-guided public opinion is the strength of the leaders. This is the dictatorship of the living Spirit of God, which gives every man the inner discipline he needs, and the inner liberty he desires.

Your security, the world's security, lies in God-control. No other social, political or economic programme goes to the root of the disease of human nature.

Only God-controlled men will make God-controlled nations to make a new world. In this adventure every man can find his vocation, every nation its destiny.'

Later, on May 29th 1938, in a speech at a reception in his honour in East Ham Town Hall, cradle of the British Labour Movement, Frank Buchman launched Moral Re-Armament.

"The world's condition cannot but cause disquiet and anxiety. Hostility piles up between nation and nation, labour and capital, class and class. The cost of bitterness and fear mounts daily. Friction and frustration are undermining our homes.

Is there a remedy that will cure the individual and the nation and give the hope of a speedy and satisfactory recovery?

The remedy may lie in a return to those simple home truths that some of us learnt at our mother's knee, and which many of us have forgotten and neglected – honesty, purity, unselfishness and love.

The crisis is fundamentally a moral one. The nations must re-arm morally. Moral recovery is essentially the forerunner of economic recovery. Imagine a rising tide of absolute honesty and absolute unselfishness sweeping across every country!

What would be the effect? What about taxes? Debts? Savings? A wave of absolute unselfishness throughout the nations would be the end of war.

Moral recovery creates not crisis but confidence and unity in every phase of life. How can we precipitate this moral recovery throughout the nations? We need a power strong enough to change human nature and build bridges between man and man, faction and faction. This starts when everyone admits his own faults instead of spot-lighting the other fellow's.

God alone can change human nature.

The secret lies in that great forgotten truth that when man listens, God speaks; when man obeys, God acts; when men change, nations change. That power active in a minority can be the solvent of a whole country's problems. Leaders changed, a nation's thinking changed, a world at peace with itself.

'We, the Re-makers of the World'- is that not the thinking and willing of the ordinary man? The average man wants to see the other fellow honest, the other nation at peace with his own. We all want to *get*, but with such changed leaders we might all want to *give*. We might find in this new spirit an answer to the problems which are paralysing economic recovery.

Suppose everybody cared enough, everybody shared enough, wouldn't everybody have enough? There is enough in the world for everyone's need, but not enough for everyone's greed.

Think of the unemployed thus released for a programme of Moral Re-Armament; everyone in the nation magnetised and mobilised to restore the nations to security, safety and sanity.

Every man, woman and child must be enlisted, every home become a fort. Our aim should be that everyone has not only enough of the necessities of life, but that he has a legitimate part in bringing about this Moral Re-Armament, and so safeguards the peace of his nation and the peace of the world.

God has a nation-wide programme that provides inspiration and liberty for all and anticipates all political programmes.

Every employed and unemployed man employed in Moral Re-Armament; this is the greatest programme of national service – putting everybody to work re-making people, homes and businesses. A Swedish steelworker told me: 'Only a spiritual revolution goes far enough to meet the needs of men and industry.'

A Labour leader said: 'I have seen the Labour Movement triumph and felt in the midst of triumph an emptiness. The Oxford Group gave my life new content. I see in its message the only key to the future of the Labour Movement and of industry the world over.'

Only a new spirit in men can bring a new spirit in industry. Industry can be the pioneer of a new order, where national service replaces selfishness, and where industrial planning is based on the guidance of God. When Labour, Management and capital become partners under God's guidance, then industry takes its true place in national life.

New men, new homes, new industry, new nations, a new world.

We have not yet tapped the great creative sources in the Mind of God. God has a plan, and the combined moral and spiritual forces of the nation can find that plan.

We can, we must, and we will generate a moral and spiritual force that is powerful enough to re-make the world."

Appendix B

ADDRESS AT GORDON'S FUNERAL
By the Rev. Alan Thornhill M. A. (Oxon)

This is a wonderful and most appropriate season to give thanks for the life of Archdeacon Gordon Hannon: the season of the Wise Men who left everything and followed the Star. In St. Matthew, Chapter 2 verse 10, it says of those men, "When they saw the Star, they rejoiced with exceeding great joy."

One of the things that struck me most when I first met Gordon, back in the early 'thirties, was of a man who rejoiced with exceeding great joy. At that time I was a young Don and Chaplain of an Oxford College; I was finding it a very challenging and difficult job. Gordon brought to me the tremendous sense of the adventure of the full Christian life, the vibrancy, the vitality of a life wholly given to God. He was then in charge of one of the greatest Parishes of the Church of Ireland. He was the youngest Archdeacon in the Church. There were literally thousands of people directly connected with this Church, there was a whole raft of Sunday Schools. Everything was organised, as he would say, "down to the last baby"!

And yet, there was something more to discover, a new dimension in his ministry. It was a Star, an Absolute in God's sky – God's absolute moral standards, something onto which you could fix your sights and find a new direction for your life. Gordon had accepted the challenge to follow that Star and make it a guide for every day of his life.

Hilda told me only this morning that in the six months that followed this discovery, sixty fresh people in his parish entered into an entirely new experience of Christ. This, she said, was what gripped her. Before, she had loved Gordon devotedly, but his faith had meant nothing to her. She was not interested in being 'good', but she was interested in helping people, and it was when she saw what was happening in the lives of people, that she decided to join her husband in his faith and commitment.

I was talking the other day with a lady from Ireland. "I was a girl of nineteen," she said, "when I first met Gordon, back in those early days. I was not much use then for faith or the Church. He made me see the thrill and adventure of the Christian life. It meant a passionate interest and concern for every individual, irrespective of nation or creed, of race or point of view. It was all intensely personal, yet at the same time, so big, seeing each individual in the perspective of God's plan for the whole nation and the whole world. It was all such fun," she added, "so full of joy." So she, too, like so many others who met Gordon, had found the Star and has followed it ever since.

But that is not the full story. In the next verse of the Bible account of the Wise Men are these words: "And when they had opened their treasures, they presented unto Him their gifts."

Gordon was a man of great gifts, gifts of mind and body, of leadership and of position. There was little in the way of prestige or preferment that might not have been his. But the time came when he 'opened up his treasures'; he went to the Primate of his Church and said, "I feel I am meant to be free of parish responsibilities, free of position, even of salary, and devote myself in the work of Moral Re-Armament, to the whole of Ireland and to countries beyond." The Primate gave his blessing and said "Yes". Perhaps he was thinking of the great tradition of Irish Christianity from the earliest days, of Irish saints and scholars and missionaries, who took the faith not only to their own land, but over the seas to Scotland, to my country, England, to the continent of Europe and out to the world. Let us never forget what Ireland has given, and gives still, to the world. Gordon Hannon was in that great tradition.

Gordon, together with Hilda, his devoted partner for fifty-five years, worked for God in sixteen countries. In Africa, they helped to plan and bring about, in Lusaka, the first great inter-racial Christian conference held in our times on that continent. Their son Peter carries on that work today. It could be said that Gordon brought the world to Ireland and Ireland to the world. Through it all he cared for people. As someone has said, "He was a father to us all."

What has it all achieved? In one way, we can talk about this all day, each of us bringing out our memories and our gratitude. In another way, we can never know the full outreach. Achievement is not the real point. Obedience, faithfulness, following the Star, is. To suggest the outreach of his life, you would need to take into account the continuing influence of his six Christian children, in different parts of the world, each of them with a Christian wife or husband, and bringing up a new generation of grand-children in the same faith.

You would have to mention fresh miracles in South Africa, among black and white and coloured alike. You would have to think of prisoners in Long Kesh switching on the radio at the end of the day, and hearing, night after night, a son of Gordon's reading the Bible, simply and beautifully, as he did today. You would have to think of a family in America, in good times and in hard, reaching out to help other people who are in great distress. You would think of work in an English University; or again, of a great Parish in Derry, where another son of Gordon's is used to bring healing to sorrow and bitterness, to strengthen faith and to fight for unity in harsh and difficult times. You would think, too, of a new home near Belfast, where the same work that Gordon pioneered goes on today. This is all just a part of the great army of men and women, known and unknown, whom Gordon influenced and who follow still. There are those whom he won, and those whose consciences he stung. All are part of the outreach of his life.

No, it is not for us to evaluate at all. The important thing about those Wise Men turns out not to be their wisdom. There are plenty of wise men in history, and plenty of stupid men, too! The thing about the first Wise Men was that they stuck to following the Star. It was not the costliness of their treasures that mattered: the world is full of treasures. The important thing is that they opened their treasures and gave them. They saw, they followed, they found, they gave, they departed. And the world sings of them and remembers them forever.

So you might say the same of our beloved Gordon. He saw, he followed, he found, he gave and now he has departed. "They departed into their own country another way." Gordon has departed to the true Country where he belongs, another way. We cannot follow him yet, but we will one day. He would say to us, I think, "Follow the Star, the absolute. One hundred per cent. The good can be the enemy of the best. Above all, rejoice with exceeding great joy."

Appendix C

Reunion

In March 1998, for the first time since 1958 in Rostrevor, Gordon and Hilda's six children met together in the same place at same time.

Outside Peter's home, The Fort House, Dundooan, Coleraine, Co. Antrim.

From the left :- Michael, who married Rosemary Howard (1971),
David who married Joan Conn (1960), Leslie who married Pat Smale (1951),
David Howden Hume who married Ruth (1971), Peter who married Lady Fiona Graham (1966),
and Brian who married Maeve Butler (1964).